GARY PAULSEN

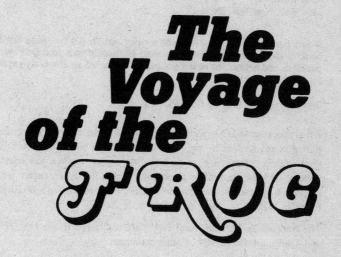

The Voyage of the FROG

A YEARLING BOOK

Published by
Bantam Doubleday Dell Books for Young Readers
a division of
Bantam Doubleday Dell Publishing Group, Inc.
1540 Broadway
New York, New York 10036

ISBN: 0-440-40364-2

Reprinted by arrangement with Franklin Watts. Inc., on behalf of Orchard Books

Printed in the United States of America

November 1990

40 39 38 37 36 35 34

OPM

For Penny Parker,
with love

Contents

The FROG

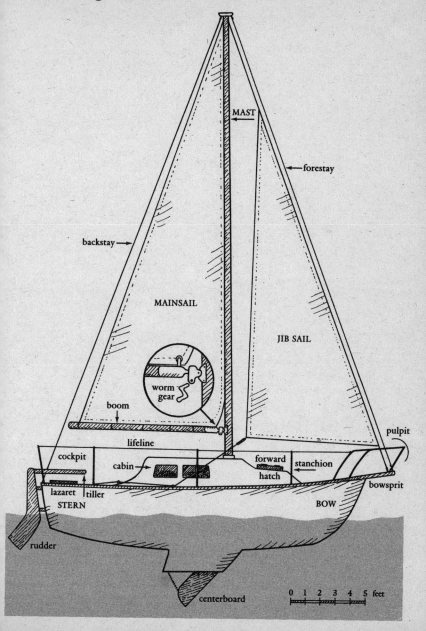

MAST

forestay

backstay

MAINSAIL

JIB SAIL

worm gear

boom

lifeline

pulpit

cockpit

cabin

forward hatch

stanchion

lazaret   tiller

STERN

BOW

bowsprit

rudder

centerboard

0 1 2 3 4 5 feet

Only the young have such moments.

JOSEPH CONRAD

The Shadow Line

1

David Alspeth stopped at the locked gate, felt in his hands the weight of the small box which he could not stand to see yet, looked down on the sailboat, and tried not to cry.

She was twenty-two feet long, with a two-foot wooden bowsprit sticking from her nose, a stainless steel pulpit above it. Her mast and boom were made of wood, kept in good shape and varnished to a high sheen. And she had stainless steel lifelines all around and a small cabin in the middle with two plastic portholes on each side.

She was old, designed by a man named Schock and made in the mid-sixties, so old her fiberglass hull had lost its shine and had a faintly sanded, opaque look to it, although the original color—a robin's-egg blue—still shone in the California sun. She had been made before they fully understood fiberglass and learned they could make it thin, so her hull was a full half inch thick, and somehow it made her look stout—tough and short and low and punchy and stout.

Across her stern was a wooden plaque and on it was hand carved *FROG*.

David ran his hand over his face. The *Frog*, he thought—and she's mine. I'm fourteen years old and I've got my own sailboat, my own complete sailboat and I would give everything, all that I am, to not have it. He looked out across the small marina that comprised most of the Ventura harbor.

There was a stiffening breeze kicking up the waves beyond the breakwaters and he smiled thinking of what his uncle Owen called waves.

"Lumps," he used to say when they were getting ready to go out and the wind was blowing the sea around. "The ocean is full of lumps. . . ."

And there it was—*used to say*. His uncle Owen didn't say anything now. Not anymore. His uncle Owen was dead. Oh God, he thought—this just stinks. It just stinks to have it be this way. He cradled the wooden box in one hand and pulled a plastic card out of his back pocket and looked at it.

It was a Ventura marina lock card made out to Owen Alspeth. He put the card in the slot next to the gate, heard the lock click, pulled the gate open. The tide was out and the walkway sloped down at a steep angle so that he had to hold the handrail to keep from trotting forward.

At the bottom the dock was flat, and he walked to the slip holding the *Frog*. She wasn't locked. Owen didn't believe in locks, didn't believe in anything that held or confined things.

"If they're going to steal something the lock won't stop them," he'd said. And nobody had ever stolen from him, though other boats in the marina had been hit several times. Didn't believe in locks or chains or tying things down. Ahh, David thought and he shook his head and tried to shake his grief, the memory of the whole stinking mess pouring back into his thoughts.

Owen had felt a backache and gone to the doctor on a Monday morning and by Tuesday he knew he was going to die, knew that the cancer he had would kill him, that they could do nothing. Nothing for him. Again David controlled the tears. Down the dock a bit an older man stared at him for a moment, then turned away.

It had spread so fast. The cancer—so incredibly fast. A week after he'd gone into the hospital they had found more tumors in his brain and Owen called

David in to visit him. David had wanted to go sooner but while they were running tests Owen had asked him to wait. David's parents—Owen was his father's brother—were taking turns staying with him in the hospital. His mother had been there when David came the first time, and Owen had asked her to leave.

David hated hospitals, and it was worse when he saw Owen lying in bed. He looked weak, caved in, dead already, dead and done, and when David saw him he was overwhelmed with the change. His uncle's cheeks were sunken and his whole face was cast in a gray that somehow looked even and flat. And the smell from him was a mixture of alcohol and urine and feces—David had heard his mother say that the tumor in his spine kept him from controlling himself from the waist down.

Instantly, without a single thought that it was coming, David threw up, and of course that made it all the more horrible. Owen, his Owen who was so close, his own Owen who had taken him out sailing so many times and who always kept himself so neat that when the wind blew his hair didn't move, his own sweet uncle Owen—and he couldn't see him without throwing up, making a mess all over the floor. To make it still worse Owen laughed. A skull laugh.

"Some smell, isn't it?"

And David thought, What can I say? What words

can come out now to make this all right? And of course nothing came and he stood there with the mess on his shirt and the floor, looking but trying not to stare, hurting and trying not to breathe, and he was taken by such a roar of hate that it made his vision blur even more than the tears.

There had to be somebody to hit for this, he thought—there had to be some damn enemy to hit for this, this stinking death thing that was in the room.

"They think I might make two more weeks," Owen said, shrugging, his bony shoulders like two hooks. Tubes seemed to be poked into him in many places and they rattled when he moved. "I doubt I'll make a week but who am I to know?"

David shook his head—angry jerks. "Don't talk like that, dammit. Things happen. People make it. There are things they can do. There are always things they can do. . . ."

But they both knew that the doctors could do nothing, could take nothing more from him nor add anything to him to save him.

"All they can do now is keep me drugged up and comfortable." Owen looked past David, out the window at the hills in back of Ventura. The smog-haze was thickening and the rolling, brush-covered hills were bathed in yellow muck. "I want you to have the *Frog*."

Another violent shake. "No. I can't take her. Not like this, not this way. You love that boat, you live for it. . . ." David trailed off, paused, finished lamely. "I just can't. It wouldn't be right."

Owen turned a dial on a small box at the edge of the bed. A tube ran from the box to a needle that entered his arm. He had a pinched look at the corners of his eyes, from the pain, but it lessened almost instantly. "It's a drug computer," he said, sighing. "It drips morphine into me and I can turn it up when the pain waves up. That's all there is now for me, little victories like that. I can turn a dial and soften pain. My whole life has come down to that. . . ."

Another silence. David was crying openly now, thinking of Owen. Once he had seen Owen dancing at a beach party with a heavy girl, and he had picked her up and held her while he danced in the sand, holding her like a feather, laughing, his arms and legs strong and tight, and now . . . now he seemed about to break from the weight of the sheets. Owen reached slowly to the nightstand next to the hospital bed, the increased drug dosage hitting him, and David saw now that there was a small envelope there. Owen scrabbled for it with his boned fingers, caught it, and handed it to David.

"Here is the title, signed over to you. You know how hard it is to find a notary public in a hospital? And the marina card is there. I think she still has some water in the tank, and there are some cans of food I left from my last trip to Catalina. I need a favor from you."

"Anything." And he meant it. I will die for you if it will save you. Anything.

"I am going to be cremated. I want you to take my ashes out alone on the *Frog*, out to sea alone, and leave me there. Take me to where you can't see land and scatter my ashes there on the water. . . ."

David held the envelope crushed in his hand, held it while he cried and the silence had come again, come and stayed and grown until David's mother came back into the room and broke it with talk.

He didn't make a week.

Just six days. On the fifteenth of May, while David was in his last day of school in the eighth grade, his uncle Owen died in a drugged state resembling a coma. Even knowing it was coming hadn't helped. The grief tore at David and his parents. Owen had no other family, had never married and had stayed close to them, lived only four blocks away, ate with them and was the first to take David sailing. Several times he had taken him on two- and three-day trips out to Santa Cruz Island and once to Catalina, and now he was suddenly gone.

Completely gone.

David stepped on the boat, felt her rock quickly to his weight, jerking lightly against the ropes that held her to the slip-dock. Seagulls had been perching on the boom; there was a mess on the top of the cabin and the floor of the cockpit, and he stepped to the side to miss it.

He unhooked the hasp holding the sliding cabin top hatch in place and slid it forward. His nose was immediately filled with the rank odor from inside the boat. The cabin hadn't been opened since the last time Owen had come to the marina, over a month ago, and it smelled of mustiness and mildew and fungus and something else as well, something David could not pin down at first.

When it came, finally, it stopped him cold, one hand on the top of the hatch. It was the smell of Owen. No. More than that. It was Owen himself. The ghost of Owen. The smell was the boat and Owen, and David could not tell in his mind where the boat ended and Owen began.

He sat then, on the edge of the cockpit, holding the box, and cried and cried, letting it roll out of him in uncontrollable heaves, his hands clasped between his knees and the sound of the waves and gulls and sea around him.

He wasn't sure how long he sat, crying silently in the cockpit, but it was probably at least half an hour. It was late afternoon, and a commercial fishing boat came into the harbor, which caused the gulls to flock in back of the boat looking for the bait the crew would throw over the stern as they docked. The sound of the gulls wheeling and squawking wildly caught David's attention, snapped him out of it, and he shook his head again, stood.

He removed the three boards that dropped in the rear slot of the main cabin door, so that it was not only open at the top but the rear as well, and swung down into the boat. The smell was still there although now it was more of mold and mustiness. He stopped and looked at the cabin.

She was, in reality, a small boat. Two steps came down from the cockpit to the cabin floor. Directly in the middle, in front of him, was a table with drop leaves on each side. On each side of the boat, facing the table, was a bench with a cushion which could also be used as a short bunk. Up front, peaked into the bow, was a double bunk filled with bags of sails—six of them. To his right and back under the cockpit was a single bed—what Owen called the captain's bunk—and to the left and under the cockpit was a storage area. David wedged the small box he held onto a shelf above it.

Under all the bunks except the forward double one were bins for more storage—no wasted space on a boat—and under the double was a water tank which David thought held twenty gallons. He couldn't remember how much exactly Owen had told him, and somehow it was very important to remember everything Owen had said. Twenty gallons, maybe. They had been sitting at Fries Cove on the island of Santa Cruz and Owen had said how important fresh water was to the old sailing ships. . . .

Then they had put masks on and gone over the side and Owen had shown him two abalone stuck to a rock and he'd popped them loose with a screwdriver and brought them up and cleaned them and fried them in butter—real butter—and David had never tasted anything so wonderful. . . .

Memories. Somehow the good ones cut the worst. The sweeter the memory the more it hurt. Stupid how that worked. He shook his head again, looked to the boat.

Down and to his right there was a small sink and alcohol stove and on the left a stand with drawers in it and a tiny cutting board on top. And that, he thought, was that. Seven feet wide at the widest and maybe twenty feet long inside, if you counted the storage space under the cockpit.

On the back of the cockpit, sealed off from the inside of the boat and only reachable from the outside, was a small hatched compartment called a lazaret, which housed the outboard motor, a five-gallon gas tank, and a battery. Owen hated the motor—sneered and called it "a cast-iron mainsail"—and David had never seen him use it. Not once.

Over the front bunk there was a forward hatch and he stepped past the table and propped it open from the inside. Air immediately began moving through the cabin and the mustiness seemed to disappear at once. He moved back to the rear and stood so that his head was out the top of the door hatch—the cabin ceiling was only four feet six inches high—and looked around at the rest of the boat.

Something in him made David want to know all about the *Frog*, some drive he did not understand, and he suddenly realized that it was the memory of Owen causing it; Owen had been so close to the boat that knowing the *Frog*, knowing all there was of her, was like seeing Owen again somehow. Owen had cared about how a boat sailed more than about how she looked—that's why the *Frog* had six sails, even a spinnaker and a tough little storm trysail— and nowhere on the boat was there a cute little decal with one of those quippy sayings like, "The captain's word is law," or "Marriages performed on this boat good for duration of the voyage only."

The top of the boat, the outside, looked like Owen's as well. She was all business. Stretching from the front pulpit to a back stanchion and all around the *Frog* were stainless-steel lifelines rigged in stout stainless-steel posts. The mast was laminated spruce, a rectangle, and the boom was also spruce but attached at a right angle to the mast with a worm gear and crank arrangement so the boom could be rotated to roll down part of the mainsail in a strong wind— an action called "reefing," a way of reducing the area of the sail. He knew the crank was in the hardware drawer under the sink. In the same drawer was a sewing kit for repairing sails, another crank handle for the winches in the cockpit that tightened the jib, and some hand tools—a couple of wrenches, a pair of pliers, and a set of screwdrivers in a plastic package.

"Everything," Owen once said, "needed to sustain life."

David thought of the small box on the shelf below. Life. All that Owen had been reduced to a small container of ashes. Life.

He moved forward in the cabin again and took the sail bag labeled MAIN and carried it up top. On deck he opened the bag and pulled at the stiff Dacron cloth until it billowed out—it also smelled musty—and he started the fasteners up the track on the mast, heaving down on the halyard, the rope that hoists the mainsail, as he added each fastener to the track.

As he pulled them up he also pulled the bottom edge fasteners out along the boom—and put the stiffening boards, the battens, into the little pockets along the trailing edge of the sail—so that when it was all the way to the top of the mast it was also out on the boom. The evening breeze kicked against the sail, making it slap back and forth. He smiled, thinking of Owen again.

The slapping of the sails was called "luffing," and Owen said it was one of the few words that sounded just like what it meant. They had been sitting at the dock, joking and drinking Cokes, and the comment triggered a whole string of words that sounded like what they meant until, finally, David looked up just as a pelican let go down the side of the mast and he said, "Poop"—which led Owen to mention that the back of the boat was sometimes called the poop deck. He wasn't sure but it was probably because they used to go to the bathroom over the stern, and the thought set the two of them off into making conversations actually using all those words they could that sounded the way they meant. . . .

Ashes. Not life now, but ashes.

David let loose the ropes—sheets—that held the boom so the mainsail could luff easily and went below for the jib. He clambered up onto the bow and clipped the snaps of the jib sail to the forestay—the cable that runs from the tip of the bowsprit up to the top of the mast—and hooked the top, or head, of the sail to the jib halyard and pulled it up. The jib was loose, without the benefit of a boom to hold the bottom edge stiff, and it slapped mightily in the wind, like a wild white rag. Now the boat was all noise, with wind luffing the sails and the boom slamming back and forth and the sails popping, ropes whipping and clacking, and the halyards slapping against the mast: whap, whap.

The sounds somehow made the boat feel urgent, as if she were impatient to go and David knew then that he was going to take her out. He took a moment and put a life jacket on, buckling it on tightly. He had told his parents he'd be spending the night on the boat in the marina, then sailing out the next day to leave Owen's ashes in the sea. And when he put the sails up he simply had in mind that he'd air them, then drop them and tie them off until morning. But all that was different now. There was a fair breeze and no clouds in sight and it seemed to be perfect for a night sail. He had only a few times sailed out at night with his uncle, but he knew that it was Owen's favorite time to sail and this was Owen's trip.

His last trip.

When the sails were up and the halyards cleated off to the base of the mast, he closed the front hatch, secured it from the inside, unsnapped the line that held the tiller, or helm, over to the side, and jumped off onto the dock. It took him a minute to uncleat the four lines that held the *Frog* in her slip and throw them down inside the cabin. Then he pushed her gently backward until she was sliding well away from the dock, jumped aboard, and pushed the tiller sideways.

She was moving very slowly, the wind pushing her a bit and adding to the movement David had started by giving her a nudge, and when he held the tiller over, it swung her stern around so she lay side-to the wind in the large open area to the rear of the slip. The mainsail and jib were both still luffing, but he grabbed the mainsheet and pulled the sail in until it filled, and the *Frog* responded almost instantly by nosing forward. He cleated the sheet off, grabbed the jib sheet, and pulled the jib in until it filled too. The *Frog* jumped up to a speed of four and a half knots.

It was a graceful, clean, neat, silent maneuver. Owen had taught him to sail from the dock before he let him sail in the open. Most people used their motors to get out of the marina, firing them up in the slip and backing out with great noise and smell—that's how Owen put it. "A great noise and smell . . ."

But he had made David learn the feel of the boat, learn to ease her backward out of the slip gently, silently, then let the sails fill and move forward effortlessly. "She's made to move with the wind," Owen would say, "made to feel the wind and move with it. The motor is an insult."

The wind was perhaps twenty knots now—perfect for driving the *Frog* at maximum speed and comfort—and as he turned toward the harbor breakwaters and mouth, moved her nose up into the direction of the wind a bit, he noticed that the wind came directly across his beam, straight from the north as he headed west out of the harbor. It was a beam reach, the fastest way to sail—across the face of the wind—and he tuned the mainsail and jib to make the curved bellies of power that meant they were using as much of the wind as possible.

The *Frog* responded like a thing alive. She fairly jumped forward in the smooth water of the marina. David brought her up a bit more into the wind as he sailed between the two breakwaters made of huge stones, two retaining walls that stuck out into the ocean. Across the front of the two walls, to block the seas from entering the harbor, was another retaining wall of boulders. He brought the *Frog* out to sea holding her to the "high" side of the harbor mouth—the upwind, northward side—to give himself as much room as possible to clear the cross-wall.

As he came to the opening he brought her downwind a bit, let the sails out a hair, and the *Frog* slipped cleanly beyond the harbor and into the open sea.

Immediately the swells took her. In the marina the water was like a lake, sheltered and placid, but as soon as the *Frog* cleared the retaining walls she took the full Pacific Ocean head on. David could never get over the size of it, the feel of the swells. All of the land masses of all the earth could fit easily into the Pacific and there would still be plenty of water left. It was staggering. Storms from China mixed with storms from Alaska, and power from those storms mixed in turn with storms from Australia, and the swells, the movement of water from all of those places, came to the coast of California— across thousands and thousands of miles. Swells from other continents, from other worlds, came under the *Frog* now as she cleared the breakwaters, and David thought again, or still, of Owen.

Every time they cleared the harbor, or every time that David was with him, Owen had become silent, looking out at the sea. It was a silence of thought, almost of reverence, a kind of worship, and David now did the same, felt the same. The sea coming under the *Frog*, the huge swells—sometimes towering twenty feet above the cockpit, that slid like oil under the boat and brought her sliding up, over, and down into the next swell—were like friendly mountains of water. They were not storm-driven waves. David had never seen those, because Owen had always carefully checked the weather before taking him on trips, but he had heard of them: storm waves that tipped whole ships over and drove them underwater.

These swells were more like a rising in the water, a lifting that seemed to come from the earth itself, as if a hand were cradling and holding the *Frog.*

And the smell was different as well. In the harbor there was the stink of living, the smell from the other boats, the smell from cars driving by.

As soon as the *Frog* cleared the harbor the wind

brought the smell of the sea, the full-rich smell of the Pacific across the boat and it was like a bath, a bath in new wind.

It was close to dusk now. The sun was just above the horizon out ahead of the *Frog*, and David eased her off the wind a bit more, letting the sails out enough to keep them bellied well, and pointed the bowsprit straight at the sun. He checked the compass and saw that he was sailing just south of west—close to 250 degrees—and he mentally noted the direction. Slightly to his right and out ahead about fifteen miles were Anacapa Rocks and Santa Cruz Island, and he wanted to miss them with room to spare.

If he ran a line just south of the channel islands and rocks, there was nothing until the Philippines, nothing until Japan but ocean, and that was where Owen wanted to be.

Take me out alone, Owen had said, until you can't see land, and leave me there. . . .

And he would do it. A night sail for Owen would be perfect. By dawn the *Frog* should be well out of sight of land, well out to sea.

David did some further mental calculations. He was making seven knots, about nine miles an hour. If he held it for ten hours he'd be ninety miles out at dawn. He hadn't checked the weather and felt vaguely unsettled about that because the *Frog* didn't have any radio gear except a cheap little transistor battery-powered receiver that hardly ever worked right. So he couldn't listen for weather reports. But it was a good boat and there didn't seem to be any bad weather coming—the evening sky was clear and the wind steady.

He would sail a line at 250 degrees, west into the Pacific, a line west for Owen into the night.

He would sail till morning and while he was sailing, holding a true line for Owen, he would think of his uncle, think of all that Owen had been to him.

A chill took him and he lashed the tiller over with the tail of the mainsheet and went below for a moment to get his windbreaker. When he came up the sun was setting. Just that fast. Directly in front of the *Frog* the sun seemed to boil down into the sea— almost as fast as it took to think of it—and as it sank it cut a reddish-golden beam across the sea, a golden path that came from the sun across the sea to splash its light against the *Frog*, against David's face as he slid the cabin hatch closed and settled at the helm again.

It was so beautiful it took his breath away, and he thought that it was like a path for the boat.

No, not the boat—it was a path for Owen. A golden path for Owen.

David smiled. Owen would think it was so hokey, so stupid to think that. He hated schmaltzy stuff like that, hated omens.

But it was there; the gold was there ahead, calling. And David hunkered next to the tiller and held the *Frog* on course and thought, hokey or not, he would follow it.

Follow it into the night.

It was about two in the morning when the light appeared from the sea. He had heard of it but had never seen it, and if he had not seen it now he would not have believed it.

David had sat awake through the long hours of the night, past midnight, sailing steadily. The wind had not changed either in force or direction, and he had held the tiller over, held her on a broad reach through the night and thought of Owen, thought of all the things his uncle had been. Somehow it made a large part of the grief lift to think that way as the *Frog* cut the calm sea, moved up to eight knots and held speed hour after hour, creaming west into the ocean. He did not think of distance, did not think of anything but Owen—

Owen sitting at the helm, in the same place David sat now, telling him what he really wanted to be, wanted to do. Nobody else knew. Not even David's parents. He had spent his whole life working one job to the next, working construction, clerking, getting by, but what he really wanted to do was study.

Just that. Study.

"I want to know all the things I don't know," he'd said, sailing in the bright sunshine on a summer afternoon.

"You mean about the sea," David had said.

Owen had nodded. "But not just the sea. All of it. I want to know all of everything there is to know that I don't know. I want to know about other planets and I want to know about molecules. I want to know about art and science and music and love and hate and dreams and trees. I want to know everything. . . ."

"But that's impossible." And David had thought then how much he hated to study, hated the whole process of school. It was a drudge to him. Something to get through.

Owen had held his hand up and told him a joke about an engineer and a pure mathematician. On one side of a room was a beautiful woman, on the other side the engineer and the mathematician. Each man would be allowed to advance half the distance to the woman each time he moved. The mathematician said that it was senseless to try because in theory you would never reach her, but the engineer smiled and said, "You can get close enough."

Owen had laughed. "It's the same with studying, with knowing things. Maybe I can't learn it all. But maybe I can get close enough. I knew a guy named Elwood back before you were born. He lived here and spent his time learning the beach at Ventura. Just here. A short stretch of public beach. The most explored beach probably in the world. But he studied and worked at it and found four new kinds of oysters—named Elwood Oysters One, Two, Three, and Four—and an undiscovered kind of octopus. Right here on the beach where there wasn't supposed to be anything more to know."

Owen. Sailing through the night David thought of Owen wanting to know things, all things, and a part of his brain kept pushing tiny warnings at him but he didn't heed them—quick little thoughts about the distance he had come, or was going to go—short thoughts about mistakes he had made, or was making. Again he thought of the weather, but only briefly, casually. He thought that he hadn't checked provisions of water, but he dismissed the notions because he wouldn't be out long. Just out and back. He should be back in the marina by evening, if the wind held.

Tiny thoughts. If the wind held.

And at two in the morning he saw the light in the water. He saw it first to the stern. In his wake, in the silent bubbles left by the *Frog* moving through the water, there was a rippled, dotted line of eerie light glowing up from the water. It was blue-green, seemed to come from down in the water, and at first it startled and frightened him. But then he remembered hearing about it.

Small animals in the water, microscopic organisms, sometimes phosphoresced—gave off light almost like lightning bugs—when disturbed. He must be going through a mass of them. In back of the *Frog* was a long line of blue light, fading as the water settled down again.

He tied the tiller off, leaned over the side, and looked toward the front where the bow cut a wave that curled over.

"Ohhh . . ." It slipped out of his mouth unbidden, almost a sigh of amazement. The boat was moving through blue fire, blue fire in the night. The bow wave was a rolling curve of blue light, sparkled with bits of green that seemed to want to crawl up the side of the boat and then fold back and over, splashing out in ripples and droplets of light.

It could not be as beautiful as it was—not be that beautiful and be real. It was so bright and shining a thing that the *Frog* seemed to be moving through, a lake of cold fire, and as he watched he saw a form move beneath the boat, caught in the blue glow of the bow wave, a torpedo form that shot forward with an incredible burst of speed. He saw first the glowing curved line around the head of the creature and the line showed him that it was the front of a dolphin. All in seconds, in short parts of seconds, he saw the head and the body moving forward beneath the boat and then it exploded—the dolphin blew out of the water in front of the boat.

It rose in a clean curve just in front of the bowsprit, five, six feet out of the water in a leap of joy that only dolphins can make, carrying with it a shroud of splashing blue-green fire that whirled and spiraled in the darkness to follow the dolphin up, over and down, back into the water and plunging in green light back to the depths beneath the *Frog*.

David was frozen with it, did not know how long he stayed with one hand reaching up as if to touch where the dolphin had been, touch the curve of blue fire. It was all there and gone—just as suddenly gone as if it had never been—and his breath burst suddenly out into the night.

He looked back, expecting to see the dolphin as the boat went over it but there was nothing. Not a trace. Only the flickering blue lights of the *Frog*'s wake. And it came to him then, came to his mind like the leaping dolphin came to his eyes, why Owen—who found such beauty in life—wished to end his days amidst the leaping dolphins and the blue fire and the lines of sun-gold across the water. The mother sea. Beginning and end.

David looked up at the sails. There was a sliver of a moon above the horizon, enough to make a pale light, and the white of the sails caught it, gathered it and shone it down on him. He was bathed in the cold, white light of the moon, washed and bathed in it. The trailing edge of the main was luffing a bit and he sheeted it in to clean the line up. That loosened the opening between the mainsail and the jib sail so he pulled the jib in a bit to clean that and the boat picked up speed.

There were several hours to daylight, two at least, maybe a bit more before the sky started to grow light. He wasn't sure how far he'd come, but when he looked back toward land he could see flickering lights above the horizon—probably lights in the mountains—so he wasn't far enough out yet.

He looked at the compass again. The numbers glowed only faintly in the darkness, but he could see them, and he was still holding at 250 degrees. Hours before, he had moved past the islands, felt more than saw them in the darkness, and headed into the open sea.

It was, really, the first time he had ever moved into the wide ocean.

With Owen he had sailed to Catalina and anchored and they had covered a fair distance—perhaps fifty miles—of sailing to get there. But it wasn't the same, still wasn't at all the same as heading into the open sea where there was not a tourist island waiting. They had always been within sight of land, and Catalina itself was only twenty-six miles from the city of Los Angeles.

It was true, David knew—they had talked of it many times while sailing—that only the water around your boat counted and you could get in as much trouble one mile from shore as a thousand miles out. A quick wind squall could dump you in sight of the harbor and the waves could hold your head down and that would be it—all in sight of the yacht club restaurant.

That was all true.

But to head into the open sea, into the wide reaches of the Pacific—away from and out of sight of land—was completely different and it sobered him now as he settled back into the business of sailing the *Frog*.

There was still a long way to go.

5

At nine in the morning he eased off on the tiller, let the bowsprit come up into the wind, and the *Frog* slowed to a standstill. The sails immediately began luffing loudly, slapping back and forth in the breeze. The sky was almost clear, with small, fluffy bits of clouds moving across the blue, and he shrugged his shoulders to ease the stiffness. He had sailed, straight on course, thinking of Owen and the art of sailing and getting the most from the wind, for just over fifteen hours, and his shoulders and arms were sore from pulling against the wooden tiller handle.

Without the push of the wind holding her over,

the *Frog* almost wallowed in the water. The change in the boat, in the whole boat, was amazing to him. When she was sailing it was as if everything mattered; everything was full and pulling, steady and taking the seas. But the instant she stopped sailing it was as if she'd turned into a fat pig. The boom jerked back and forth, ropes flopped like sick snakes, the sails looked sloppy and loose, and she rolled from side to side on the smallest swell or wave like an old washtub.

He had come far enough. He stood and looked in all directions and could see no land, nor plane, nor other boat, no indication that there was another human on the planet. Rather than lying flat, though it was only a mild breeze the sea seemed to rise around and away from the *Frog*. It was as if she lay in the middle of a huge slate-blue saucer or dish that went up and away on all sides to the horizon.

There was a thing to do. He let the tiller hang—the *Frog* was locked "in irons," her head up into the wind, and would not be going anywhere. The cabin again smelled a bit of mustiness, and he opened the forward hatch and propped it open on its brace, felt the breeze come scooping in and clear the boat out.

It had been a cool night, but the morning sun was getting hot and he took off his windbreaker, put it on the captain's bunk—he couldn't help thinking "Owen's bunk"—and turned back to the rear of the boat, stopped next to the galley area. The box with Owen's ashes was still on the shelf to his right. He caught himself pointedly not looking at it.

There was a thing to do and he knew it but did not want to do it. It was so . . . so final somehow. To put Owen into the sea . . .

The instructions had been specific. Open the box and scatter the contents. David took the small box and went back up into the cockpit. He positioned himself in the stern, one hand holding the backstay— the support cable from the top of the mast back down to the rear of the boat—and stood for a moment, looking across the water, thinking a prayer, not in words so much as a thought-prayer.

When he opened the lid of the box it was impossible not to look inside. The ashes were a gray, rubbled mass that didn't even fill the box.

All of it, he thought. All of Owen. The man who danced in the sand with the girl, the man who wanted to know all things, the man who would sit and talk to him for hours—the living man that Owen had been was an inch and a half of gray ashes in a small wooden box.

It wasn't possible.

It simply could not be.

He looked to the sky again, took a deep breath that somehow shuddered in him, and turned the box upside down over the stern. The ashes spread on the water and strangely now he did not cry but wished only to be gone.

It was done.

He turned away without looking, then as an afterthought threw the box as far as he could and did not watch where it landed with a splash. Somehow the box angered him. That they would or could put all of Owen in it angered him. All of it, the cancer, the death—all of it angered him and he wanted nothing now but to get the *Frog* underway and sail from this spot.

He pushed the tiller over hard to the left. The *Frog* was still locked in irons, head up into the wind, but she was nonetheless moving a tiny bit to the rear, and with the helm over hard to one side she would slowly back around side-to the wind again and he could get her sailing. Another thing Owen had taught him: how to do all things without the motor.

But as he held the tiller over he reached for the jib sheet to pull the sail tighter to take the wind when the boat came around, and the sheet was caught on the front hatch which he had forgotten to close.

Normally he would just drop down inside the boat and lower the hatch from inside. But one strand of nylon, a tiny strand from the jib sheet, was hooked on the top of the hatch in a screwhead and he would have to go up on the cabin to unhook it.

That one small thing, that tiny thread hooked on a screwhead, saved his life. Later he would wonder about it, about how the thread in the nylon rope came to be hooked that way—it had never happened before—and he would think on twists in his life, how something as small as a thread could save him.

He let the tiller go again and with one hand on the wooden handrail that was bolted to the top of the cabin he clambered forward, impatient to be sailing, heading home, away from this place in the sea where Owen's ashes were floating.

At the forward hatch he quickly unhooked the caught thread and dropped the hatch cover in place—it had to be fastened tightly from the inside—and stood to move back to the stern. The jib was luffing in great slaps and it hit him in the face so that he put a hand up to protect himself; that hand pushed the sail to the side and he could see forward, over the bow a great distance because he was standing, and that's when he saw it.

Away to the north, close to two or three miles distant, the swells looked strange. The sky was clear and the morning sun was off to his right. He could see well enough, but it still looked strange. It seemed as if the tops of the swells were flattened somehow. Either pushed flat or . . . or something else. What? Cut off? He stood on tiptoe—silly that, as if raising himself an extra inch or two could help, but it was automatic—and squinted. Maybe it was light, sun-light or something cutting the water off funny.

No. They truly looked different. Not flattened so much as cut. As if a giant knife were cutting the tops off the swells and waves. Without his consciously knowing it, the hair on the back of his neck moved up and his shoulders tightened. So strange. He'd never seen such a thing, never even heard of it. Owen had never mentioned anything like it.

The waves were just cut off clean.

What would cut them that way?

Wind.

The answer came with the sound—an almost quiet moan mixed with a sharp tinkling that he realized was the wind pushing water spray ahead of it in a kind of horizontal frothy rain.

It was wind. A wild wind—a wind stronger than anything he'd ever seen or heard of, a wind without warning out of the northwest. For precious seconds he stood, the cut line of swells moving toward him, stood and stared in disbelief. It just couldn't be wind. There were no clouds in the sky, no fronts coming, no signs of weather at all—yet it was there.

Like a fool, he thought, I stand like a fool. It was a wind to take him, to kill the *Frog* and he had wasted time staring. He ran for the mast and released the jib halyard. The truth is that if such a wind hit the *Frog* with all her sails up for whatever reason, she would be driven over and down and sunk in seconds.

The sound was louder now—a hissing moan that had an almost evil resonance to it—but he didn't waste time studying it. He clawed the jib down, wadded it in a ball and—with it still hooked to the forestay—he opened the forward hatch and jammed all of the sail he could into the opening. He pushed the hatch back down. It would not latch, but it would have to do.

No time now. Just seconds. He could smell the spray, salt moistness, being driven ahead of the storm—it must be a storm. Some freak storm. He jumped back to the mast and untied the mainsail halyard. Normally the sail would drop of its own weight, but now the wind was getting stronger—he sensed-heard the scream of it, his hair was plastered and blown over his face—and the main stayed up, held now by the pressure of the wind.

He swore, grabbed at the sail and started to rip it down. Everything was noise—the wailing of a thousand screaming throats in the wind, the slapping of the sail sounding like a cannon. He felt one of his fingernails give on a seam. He kept tearing the sail down.

The top of the hatch! He had to get the cabin top hatch open. He moved along the boom, still pulling at the main, fighting to hold himself upright in the wind, and kicked the sliding cabin top forward. The kick made him stumble, and the wind picked him up almost bodily and threw him out, away from the boat, but he tangled in the safety lifeline, caught himself and pulled back up to the cabin top.

The mainsail was slashing back and forth like a demon gone mad. He couldn't control it. Frantically he attacked, pushing part of it down into the cabin through the open top hatch only to have the wind sweep it out while he was gathering more of the billowing insanity to push down again.

It was too late. There was a momentary—part of a second—hitch in the roar of the wind, a tiny hesitation and the full force of the storm hit the *Frog* like a giant sledgehammer. David had a fraction of time to disbelieve the wind—so strong it sucked his eyelids away from his eyes and pushed the *Frog* sideways, scudding like a leaf—then he tried to lean forward for the hatch opening just as the spruce boom, fifty pounds of laminated wood and metal rail still attached to the mainsail, caught a corner of the storm and slammed across the boat like a sweeping saber.

It caught him full on in the center of the top of his head with a crack that sounded like the boom had broken.

There was an immense, staggering flash of white-red color somewhere in the middle of him—with an exploding pain that covered the whole top of his brain like a burning glove—and he knew, as he fell down and forward into the top of the open cabin hatch, he knew it was too late.

He was in a great, billowing white cloud, floating in the whiteness, and there were huge buckets of water being thrown on him. No sense to it. Screaming noise, ropes slamming against the mast, cracking of cloth being whipped or snapped—everything so loud it hurt his ears. No, not just his ears but everything, everything hurt all the time. Not just the sound, but all of it. Pain.

Pain.

Something was wrong with his head, badly wrong. He couldn't think or make his thought patterns begin to work: just swirling and the white cloud and the water on him, tons of water on him and he went under again.

Later. More pain. Not just in his head now but in his shoulder somehow, his shoulder and left arm down to his hand. Water all around. He was covered with it now, with the white cloud and water.

How could that be?

The *Frog*. He was in the *Frog*, down on the floor of the cabin of the *Frog* but something was wrong, terribly wrong. Through the jolts of pain he could almost see, almost think and there was water everywhere, too much water. The *Frog* was being driven and slammed by the waves, heeling almost on her side, pitching forward and back to a nearly vertical position and each time she was thrown by the storm, by the wind and waves, she took water in. The floor was awash with it and David lay in the water. Three, four inches of it surging back and forth with the movement. The white cloud was the mainsail, he was face down in the water and the sail which he'd fallen on.

Yeah. That was it. He was in the *Frog* and she was taking water.

Not good—he thought it that way. Not good. Have to help. Have to stop water.

The front hatch. He raised his head—a new explosion of pain—and focused on the forward part of the boat. The front hatch had come all the way open, whipped up by the jib sail when the wind hit it, and every time they took a wave, water poured into the hatch opening.

It would not be long before she foundered and sunk. She could not hold much more water without going down.

He had to get up, move forward and tighten the hatch down as much as he could with the sail still through it. Pinch it down on the sail. Stop the water. That's all there was to it. He had to do it.

He tried to get up but when he moved his left arm there was a horrid popping sensation and a new, slashing rip of pain that started with the felt-sound in his shoulder, moved down his left arm, and nearly put him out again. He took long breaths, holding his head out of the water sloshing back and forth on the floor.

I've got to close the hatch. It drummed in his brain with the scream of the wind. I've got to close the hatch. . . .

Using his right hand and arm first as a lever, he pushed the front half of his body up—fighting nausea from the rolls of pain that took him—and with a snatching motion grabbed the sink, pulled himself to a crouching position.

The boat nearly slammed him back down. Waves hit her like trucks, solidly, deeply, drove her back and down the face of them, and the motion seemed more violent when he tried to stand. Like trying to climb a living, angry mountain.

He stumbled onto the right seat cushion—somehow still in place—and pulled his way forward to the bunk in the bow. He reached up for the hatch and was driven down once more by a wave coming through which must have dumped at least fifteen gallons of new water in the boat.

Again he tried, and got a hand on the hatch handle, only to be whipped away once more by the heaving of the boat. He was running out of strength, could feel it draining from him, but on the third try he at last managed to pull with all his weight on the hatch and pinch it down around the jib sail and fasten the screw-down tighteners. Then he fell back on the bunk and was immediately dumped in the water on the floor again by the pitching of the boat. But it didn't matter now. He'd done all he could, and he curled up in a ball in the water, trying to protect his left shoulder and head at the same time and let unconsciousness take him.

Time.

He couldn't make time work right in his thoughts, indeed, couldn't make his thoughts work right at all.

Time seemed to telescope. It was dark when his eyes opened again, or partially opened. But it didn't seem to have been that long. Pitch dark, and the storm was, if anything, worse. The drawers had burst open and there were tools and plastic silverware, plates and cups floating in the water. The noise, the slamming enormity of the noise was deafening. Waves thundered and cracked when they hit the *Frog*.

He couldn't understand at first how it could be dark. It seemed that he just fell back a few moments before and now it was black night. His thoughts were jumbled, piled like the waves on each other, and he couldn't believe that it had been all day; a whole day in the storm just wasn't possible.

He could see almost nothing in the cabin. The ghostly white of the sail gave an eerie glow to the tiny space but no real light. Water moved back and forth in surges now—almost six inches deep when it sloshed against his chest.

He fumbled with his right hand and found the end of the bunk by the side of the table. There was no power in the arm and it took him four tries to pull and crawl his way up onto the bunk. He heard a faint sobbing over the shriek of the wind and for a second thought there was somebody else in the cabin, then he realized that he was doing it himself.

Animal sounds. Breath mixed with spit and fear and pain. He jammed himself back into the corner of the bunk against the sink and immediately went under again—sleep-numbness came in a drug-like release that took him down. He had a tiny thought that the *Frog* couldn't take any more of the crashing, a fleeting worry, and he was gone, spiraling down into the noise and pitching madness.

Silence.

Silence and some warmth that he didn't understand, and he thought, or felt, that he was dead and that it wasn't so bad being dead. Everything was still, and quiet, and the pain had settled to a dull throb.

Then he moved his head and almost screamed. The top of his head had been jammed back up into the corner where the side of the boat met the sink stand and when he moved it everything inside seemed to come loose. A flash of intense, jolting agony took him—overwhelming dizziness—and he passed out once more, but only for seconds, and when he came to again he opened his eyes.

"Arrghhk!" He couldn't help the sound. The sun was bright—brighter than he'd ever seen—and it cut into his eyes, into the center of his mind like a white knife. He pinched his eyes shut again, opened them slowly, just a crack, let the light in more slowly.

It was day. He couldn't say for certain what time. Sunlight streamed in through the cabin windows and slashed across the whole middle of his body. Maybe midafternoon. That was why he felt warm. His pants, still soaked, were steaming as the moisture left them where the sun cooked the fabric.

So he wasn't dead.

It just felt that way.

His temples still throbbed with the light but as he became accustomed to its sharpness he opened his eyes more and more. Carefully, without moving his head, he swiveled his eyes to look at the boat.

"God." He whispered it. The interior of the cabin was a shambles. The only cushion still in place was the one he was lying on—all the rest were tossed every which way. Everything that had been stored under the bunks had been thrown clear, which didn't make any logical sense to him. To have that happen the *Frog* must have gone almost upside down. How could she have done that without sinking?

The contents of drawers were strewn everywhere about the boat. Cans of food sloshed in eight inches of water on the floor. A roll of toilet paper was turning to white mush next to a ruined small box of sugar. Packets of tea were floating in the folds of the crumpled mainsail that hung down through the top hatch, staining the water in brown clouds. The stove had come loose from its mount and been flung across the cabin and was jammed against the wall on the opposite side.

The sail bags, which had been tucked neatly up

in the front corner of the bow, had come loose and were scattered all around, wet but seeming to be undamaged otherwise. There was . . . clutter . . . everywhere. Just junk. He hadn't thought there could be that much garbage in the boat. Bits of paper, styrofoam cups, small pieces of cardboard . . . The boat looked like a garbage scow more than anything else.

He saw all this without moving his head, letting his eyes slide back and forth. Even that effort hurt some, so when he at last had to stand—to go to the bathroom—he tried it in small stages. First a tiny movement as he pulled his head down and out of the corner, wincing with pain, then his right arm— it seemed to be the only part of him not hurt— grabbing the table to help pull him upright.

After half a minute he was sitting on the cushion, weaving a bit. The pain in his left shoulder was easing. He guessed that he must have dislocated it when he fell and that the violent action of the boat must have popped it back in.

But his head still ached across the top. He lifted a hand and was surprised to find caked blood and a raised ridge in a line across the middle. The boom had really smacked him—he was lucky it hadn't knocked him completely off the boat—but he hadn't thought it had cut him.

He pulled himself to a crouched-over, standing

position, moaning quietly, and shuffled in the water to the rear hatch, scootching around the mainsail which, hanging down, still filled the opening.

It took him a full minute to slowly get up the two steps, fight off the mainsail again, and position himself at the stern so he could go to the bathroom.

The sun and sea were dazzling. The sky was an intense blue with a hot, flat sun high overhead—he thought it might be noon but could not think of what day it was—and there was absolutely no wind. Not a breath disturbed the oily surface of the low swells that slid gently beneath the *Frog*. The water had a metallic quality to it, a steel blue in contrast to the sky and seeming to give off a light of its own that cut into his eyes.

Heavy with water, the *Frog* wallowed in the swells, had none of the quickness and lightness he was used to, and while he hung on the backstay at the stern it all hit him at once.

He was thirsty and hungry and the boat was still near to sinking and he didn't know how long the storm had lasted and didn't know where he was and didn't have a radio or even a watch, now. His digital wristwatch had lain in the water while he was unconscious and had filled and stopped—and it was supposed to be waterproof. Good to six hundred feet or something. Right.

Slowly, he opened his eyes and looked around the horizon, wincing again with the new movement. There was nothing sticking above the water as far as he could see.

He was alone.

It was not possible to think at first.

He turned back to the cabin, moving bent over like an old man, holding his sore arm and shoulder, and he simply could not think. It was enough for the moment to feel the warmth of the sun, smell the sea, see the sky. Blue life. He had been certain he was dead and suddenly there was blue life all around him and he could not make himself think of what to do.

Alone.

That was it. He was alone and the *Frog* was full of water and he was thirsty and hungry—it all rushed in again and he had to fight to stop the terror of it.

What he wanted to do most of all was panic. To scream and panic and then look up and see a rescue boat or chopper and know that it was over.

But that didn't happen.

Alone. He was alone and had to stop the thinking before panic blew up on him and he lost control. First things first. He had to pick one thing and work on it.

The storm. He knew about that. The storm had taken him, taken the boat in its fist and blown it—where? How far? He frowned, thinking. The storm had lasted, how long—a day? No, more than that. There had been that time in the darkness. The madness in the darkness. The crashing darkness. So it had been most of one day, and through the night and, he thought, into the next morning.

Twenty, perhaps twenty-four hours. And how fast had the sea been taking him?

No way to know. His head hurt to think about it. Say five knots. Maybe a bit more. Make it six knots. About seven and a half miles an hour. Too complicated. Make it eight miles an hour. The storm had been pushing him south and west at eight miles an hour for probably twenty-four hours.

A hundred and ninety-two miles.

But that wasn't all of it. He had sailed twelve hours at almost ten miles an hour before that, in the same direction, south and west. That was another hundred and twenty miles.

Say three hundred and fifteen miles, at least, southwest of the California coast, to where he sat right now, rolling heavily in a boat half full of water.

And you said not to panic, a small voice told him—why not panic? You're alone three hundred plus miles at sea in a small boat. You deserve to panic. Go ahead and panic.

Wrong thinking. He shook his head—nearly screamed at the pain it caused him—and leaned against the cabin opening. There were more demanding problems than figuring out where he was or how long it took for him to get there. The *Frog* was in trouble, still in bad trouble even though the storm was gone. She could have only four or five inches of freeboard left on the sides and, at the least heeling, her deck would go under from the weight of the water inside the boat. If that happened she'd go down like a rock.

And I'd be floating alone three hundred and fifteen miles from shore in a life jacket.

He had to pin things down and start somewhere. First a drink. His mouth was so dry and clammy his lips almost stuck together when he closed them. He moved gingerly down into the cabin, standing once more in the water, and picked up a plastic cup floating in the garbage near the sail. He was amazed to find that the hand pump on the sink still worked, although to be realistic nothing should have broken it, and he pumped the cup full four times and drank the water from the freshwater tank under the front bunk. It tasted slightly brackish, and of fiberglass, but was sweet to him anyway and did much to cheer him.

Until he thought of the water tank. He could not remember at first how large it was and he didn't know if it was full. Owen had told him once—was it twenty gallons? Twenty-two? Was that it? He'd have to check it and see how full it was because he didn't know how soon he would get more water because he didn't know how far he was, really, from shore and he was alone and couldn't expect any help and if he ran out of water he would start to drink sea water and he'd read stories about people who drank sea water going insane and dying horrible deaths. . . .

He stopped thinking again. The panic was right there, on the edge, waiting to blow everything up if he let it.

"I've got to do this thing one step at a time," he said aloud. "There has to be an order to this."

One hand for the ship—the phrase suddenly jumped into his mind. In the old sailing days of clipper ships and square riggers, when sailors had to climb up in the rigging and hang out on the wooden yards swinging wildly many feet above the deck while they worked at getting the sails squared away, new men, especially, had a hard time of it and would frequently get out on the yard, look down and freeze in terror, grabbing the yard or sail ropes, and just hang on for dear life. And to be sure, many of those old-time sailors fell to their deaths. But for others a mate down below would yell up, "One hand for the sailor, one hand for the ship." It meant of course that the sailor should let go with one hand and overcome his fear, to get the sails working.

The words applied now. One hand for the ship. The most important thing right now wasn't his fear, it wasn't his location or even how much water and food he had. It was the *Frog*. His whole life depended on the *Frog* and if he didn't take care of her—give one hand for the ship—none of the rest of it was likely to matter.

She was staggeringly heavy with the water in her. That was the first thing. He had to get the water out and get her back to floating right.

Next to the motor in the stern compartment—the lazaret—there was a small hand pump with two hoses attached to it. The idea was you put one hose into the in-board water, ran the other hose over the side, and worked the plunger handle until the water was gone.

He got the pump—was surprised to find the motor still in one piece, although there was a small dent in the square five-gallon gas can next to it—and arranged the hoses, one over the side, the other down in the water inside the cabin.

He worked the plunger once and about a half a cup of water spurted out into the ocean. Another pump. Another spurt. He hit it six or seven times really fast but the spurt didn't increase, didn't decrease, always half a cup. He sat on the cockpit seat and settled into work. Half a cup a shot meant about eight pumps to a quart of water. Thirty-two pumps to a gallon.

He studied the water down inside the cabin. It was impossible to guess how many gallons but it had to be at least a hundred. So that would be thirty-two hundred pumps of the plunger.

Pump.

Spurt.

Pump.

Spurt.

It was going to be a long day.

There were over a hundred gallons in the cabin. He pumped for a time and counted them, figuring that he worked the pump about thirty times a minute, so a hundred minutes would be three thousand pumps. A hundred minutes and there was still a lot of water in the cabin—the boat didn't even feel much lighter, still lay heavily in the shallow swells. After perhaps four hours, his right arm aching with the effort, she at last lightened; the water was a shallow puddle in the middle of the cabin floor. Another half hour and the hose was making slurping noises and he stopped. The dampness left in the floor carpet would evaporate in the sun's heat.

It was evening now, the sun low over the water. In the entire day there had not been one breath of wind, and the sails still hung where he had jammed them before the storm. He had to get them up, aired out, and stowed correctly or at least tied in place, but he found that he could not move.

His left shoulder still hurt—somehow working the pump with his right arm had aggravated the left one as well—and his head still hurt from the boom injury, but it wasn't that so much as just plain exhaustion. He felt wrecked.

She was floating right. He had given one hand for the ship and now he just simply could not move. He sat on the left seat of the cockpit and leaned against the back cabin wall and closed his eyes and sleep took him as if he'd been hit with a soft hammer.

Not long. Half an hour, perhaps a bit more—he kept looking at his watch once he was conscious but it was still blank—and he came suddenly awake. Like that. As fast as he'd gone to sleep. He had a crick in his neck from leaning against the cabin side and he stood and stretched, felt his neck pop a bit, then carefully reached and stretched his left arm. It would go shoulder high, no higher. That would have to do.

He stepped up to the side rail and moved forward to the mast. The halyards still hung loose, tangled with each other and the loosened jib sheets—Owen would have been furious if he could have seen the mess—and using mostly his right arm for the effort he untangled the ropes and pulled the mainsail back up, feeding it out of the cabin roof gently to keep it from snagging. It was sopping, but the Dacron wouldn't rot or soak up water and would dry rapidly up in the open. The air was so still that the sail hung without even gentle luffing—he had never seen it this calm, without even the customary soft breeze which Owen had told him came when the evening cool met with the day heat and caused air movement—and he cleated the halyard off easily. He went back down into the cabin and opened the front hatch to loosen the pinched jib. It took him several minutes, using only his right hand, to push the jib back out and onto the deck—he'd push up a handful and it would fall back on him. Then he went topside again and hoisted the jib, which hung as dead as the main.

The inside of the boat was still a frightful mess, with garbage and dampness all around. But the *Frog* was at least a boat again, floating high on the slick calm of the swells, her sails up and drying. . . . One hand for the ship.

Thirsty again—it came just that way. He was thirsty and he took another cup full of water from the hand pump at the sink. How could he be thirsty in the middle of the whole ocean? His mouth felt as if he'd been in a desert. One cup didn't seem to be enough so he drank another, then remembered that he didn't know how much water there was in the tank.

As soon as his thirst was pushed down, the hunger came up. He had not eaten for two days, and his stomach seemed to have turned in on itself. In the middle of the cabin floor, rolling back and forth, was a can of bite-sized ravioli. He found the can opener back under the cockpit, jammed up in the corner of the captain's bunk. When he figured the angle the boat had to roll and pitch to flip out the locked-in silverware drawer, tip it over, and dump the can opener that far away, the back of his neck stiffened with fear. She must have been well past sideways, heading for a complete rollover. It didn't seem possible for the *Frog* to have gone over that far without filling and sinking and he was almost glad he'd been unconscious when it happened.

"There are some things it's better not to know," he whispered in the cabin. "Better just to let them be. . . ."

It took him another minute to find a spoon—knives, forks and spoons were scattered all over—before he could sit down to eat. Then it was almost a religious experience. He took out each bite-sized ravioli, held it in his mouth, chewed slowly and lovingly sitting in the cockpit, then swallowed it, hesitating a moment before taking another bite. It was the first time in his life he had been really hungry. Owen and his parents had spoken of hunger, world hunger, and he had seen shows on television. But he had never really been without food for any length of time, never over a few hours. He found two things happening to his thinking—first, he became angry. There was no sense to it, but the hunger made him angry, as though it were a personal attack on him. And the second feeling was that he loved food.

Not just liked it, but loved it. It tasted so fine, the junky little can of ravioli bites, tasted so incredibly fine that it made his temples hurt while he chewed. He wanted to keep the ravioli forever, keep it and cherish it and eat it all at the same time.

He took over an hour to eat the canful. Around him the evening came down, the sun seeming to hurl itself from the western sky into the distant sea, the ocean cooling the air with the sun gone—though still without wind—until he felt the chill and went below for his jacket.

His eyes kept closing. He sat outside for a while, wishing it were not getting dark—something about the coming darkness frightened him—and his eyes kept closing.

"It's not that I'm tired," he said to himself, aloud. "Not so tired . . ." But his eyes kept closing, and finally he leaned against the cabin wall, sitting in the cockpit, and dozed again, and would have slept except that after a few minutes it became uncomfortable. He went down inside the boat and stretched out on the captain's bunk. The cushion was still sopping wet, but he didn't care any longer and was almost instantly asleep, sure that nothing would awaken him until daylight.

His eyes snapped open in the near darkness. The inside of the boat was bathed in pale, white light coming from the moon through the cabin windows and rear hatch opening. He lay still on the bunk, feeling the *Frog* ride lightly on the waves, listening intently. There was silence, complete silence, not even the sound of water working against the side of the boat—stone silence in the moonlight and no reason that he should have sprung awake the way he did.

For a time his eyes were wide open and he listened with his breath held, but when he saw nothing, heard nothing, felt nothing he closed his eyes and started to drift back off to sleep, and would have gone under except that just as his brain began to shut down the world exploded.

There was a horrible scraping sound, like somebody dragging a claw down the whole length of the boat, a sharp rake or claw, dragging it from one end to the other, and with the sudden roar of the scraping—in the boat it seemed to be magnified—the hull took a jolt that rocked the *Frog* to the side. A small jolt, then another large one, another small one, and the scraping grew fainter and was gone.

Silence again.

It had happened so fast, was so stunning that David had no time to react except to suck in half a breath and hold it in terror.

He now rolled out of the bunk, the pain in his arm and head forgotten, and scrambled through the rear hatch onto the deck. The boat rocked gently for a moment, then settled back into stillness. There was no breeze and he could see nothing floating on the water in the moonlight around her.

Silence.

He climbed up on the cabin and held the mast, stepping on both sides and studying the surface of the water. Nothing moved. Nothing showed. Nothing.

Still, he thought—still, something had been there. He hadn't dreamed it.

Or had he?

He was in that time of sleep when the mind plays tricks, just before deep sleep. Maybe that was it. Maybe it was some kind of dream or hallucination. People did that sometimes. Hallucinated. He had been half asleep and had imagined the whole thing. That had to be it.

He moved slowly back into the cockpit. There had been the scraping against the hull. Surely if that had been real it would have left some scratches in the side of the boat.

Kneeling on the edge of the cockpit seat, he hung onto the lifeline with his right hand and leaned out so that he was hanging over the water about a foot and a half above the surface, and tried peering down the side of the hull in the moonlight. The water beneath his face seemed to have a darkness of its own, a deep darkness, a whole world of darkness in its depths. At first he could see nothing but the shine of the fiberglass in the dull light. Then he refocused his eyes and squinted.

There. A line, no, there were four or five of them— scratches or gouges that went for about three feet along the side of the boat, curving sideways and down into the water. It looked as if a giant claw had come out of the water, raked along the boat and then disappeared back into the sea.

He hadn't dreamed it, and everything in him wanted it to be a dream, now that he saw the marks.

And that thought—that he hadn't dreamed about the sound and the lurching of the boat—was almost his last. Out of the corner of his eye, just below him, David caught the faintest swirl of movement in the deep shadows of the water. Later he couldn't be sure if it was truly a shadow or the water itself. But whatever it was, it gave him a slight fraction of a second's warning and he began to pull his head back.

The water detonated, surged up at his face, and a shark's gaping maw, teeth flashing in the moonlight, triangular-death-razor-sharp teeth, blew up and out of the darkness, slashed past his face in a ripping sideways motion, and savagely raked down the side of the hull, slamming against the side of the boat so hard that it knocked the *Frog* sideways.

Not over a second and it was gone. Silence. David had thrown himself backward into the cockpit and lay on his back with his head out the other side of the boat, over the water. He realized suddenly that he was exposed and jerked back to the middle to sit in wide-eyed terror, staring at the calm surface around the boat.

"Pssssoosh!" The air whistled out of his lungs. He took another deep breath and without meaning to held it for another half a minute, waiting, but nothing came, nothing made a sound.

He was shaking, his whole body trembling. Out of nowhere, with no warning, to explode that way and slash at him—or maybe not at him, but close to him—to come that way and attack the side of the boat while his head hung out over the water . . .

Like bait, he thought. I was like bait. And to think I used to dive with Owen. If it wanted me, truly wanted me, it could come right into the cockpit.

Shark. Just the word hit him then—shark. The mouth looked large enough to take his head off. Shark. When he thought of it coming out of the black depths that way, coming out of the darkness like something evil, his breath came in tight little jerks. He could think only of being taken—taken down and down into the blackness.

To be snatched off the boat and taken down and down alone, completely alone in the world, down into the inky darkness . . .

No, he thought. I have to stop this. What happened, really? It's not like *Jaws*, not really. A fish, a big fish with lots of teeth, but a fish just the same, hit the side of the boat and I happened to be leaning over the water when it hit. It might not have even been after me. I just happened to be leaning there. It could have been just hitting the boat.

Wham! As if sensing his thoughts, the shark hit again, crashing against the side of the *Frog*, pushing it sideways, ripping new fear through him. He almost screamed. But this time he controlled the fright faster and realized that he had been right. It was hitting the boat, was not after him—and while he thought of it the shark hit once more, then again, on the same side of the boat but slightly forward.

David went below into the cabin and felt the hull where the shark had hit and found there was no damage. While he was inside it struck a sixth time, still on the port—left—side of the boat just above the waterline, and he could feel the hull flex with the blow.

It didn't make any sense. He had always heard sharks were attracted to blood in the water, blood or meat or garbage, but there wasn't anything on that side of the boat to attract a shark. It was just a clean, blue-white surface. . . .

Wait a minute. He studied the moon again. It was low and over on the left side of the boat, so that the light reflected from the moon bounced off the left side of the hull and down into the water.

From below it must seem to be something flashing just on the surface of the water. And he had read someplace—no, heard it at a talk at Marineland— that sharks will sometimes hit flashing light or movement because it is similar to the flash a wounded fish makes when it rolls.

Knowledge, he thought—even as the shark hit again—is everything. As Owen had said. Owen who had wanted to know all there was.

Knowledge was for times like this, David thought, rolling with the shark attacks. To have knowledge makes anything endurable. It's everything.

The shark stayed near the boat for three more hours, hitting at more and more infrequent intervals, until the moon was straight over the mast and no light reflected from the hull. Then the attacks stopped completely and David went back to the captain's bunk to sleep the rest of the night without awakening until the morning sun baked the inside of the cabin.

9

She was still an unholy mess. It looked as though someone had dumped a couple of garbage cans inside the cabin. And the cushions were so wet they still squished when he moved on them. His back and side were soaked from sleeping on sopping foam, his left arm so wet it had wrinkles in it, as if he'd stayed in a bathtub too long.

He stood with his head out the top of the cabin hatch and stretched, noted that his arm could reach higher than it had the day before, and looked to the sky, a flat blue that seared down to the slate blue of the ocean, rolling still and slick and dead. Out at the horizon it was impossible to see the line where the sea and the sky met, and he felt once more as if he were in the bottom of a large blue bowl. No wind. No, he thought, make that *still* no wind.

There was a worse than bad taste in his mouth—as if all night he'd been sucking on his feet, he thought—and he had no toothbrush. He turned automatically to the sink to get water to rinse his mouth out but thought better of it. Fresh water was precious, much too important to spit out.

Jammed up in the forward peak, where the water and wave action had taken it, was a plastic bucket. He retrieved it, found some thin line tangled in a ball, and untangled enough to cut and tie ten feet to the handle of the bucket.

He threw it over the side and pulled half a bucket of sea water back to the cockpit. He couldn't help standing well back from the side, remembering the shark, though he knew, or felt sure, it had just been striking at the reflected moonlight. He shuddered, remembering the teeth raking the side of the boat.

In a small drawer near the floor under the sink—the only drawer that hadn't flown open and scattered its contents all over—he found a washrag. Topside again, he stripped down and carefully bathed his whole body. The cockpit was a small well with two drainholes at the back, not unlike a bathtub, and he washed and rinsed repeatedly, refilling the bucket several times by throwing it over the side and holding it above his head to dump it like a shower.

It was the first time he had actually taken an inventory of himself and he was amazed at the number of bruises. There were long, lateral raking bruises down the sides of his ribs, blue-black lines that didn't hurt but looked as if they should. Then more splotches of blue on his hips and the insides of his legs—these ached dully—and a welt-bruise across his stomach. He washed carefully, the saltwater stinging gently when he hit a scratch or small cut—there seemed to be many of them as well as bruises. He rinsed the rag and dabbed at the cut on his head where the boom had taken him.

The storm must have been even more violent than he'd imagined. It must have hammered and thrown him around inside the cabin when he was unconscious—there could be no other explanation for all the bruises and cuts.

Salt in wounds, salt water in wounds, was supposed to help them heal. Hurt but heal. He'd read that somewhere. Oh yes, now he knew. They used to whip men, he remembered the story suddenly—the British navy used to tie men to the rail and flog them with a cat-o'-nine-tails, a whip made of nine leather strips, each with a small pellet of lead tied to its end. He'd read a story in one of Owen's sailing books. Just for drinking too much fresh water a man could be flogged with the cat-o'-nine-tails. Each time the whip struck, it would make cuts and lay the man's back bare—a vicious punishment from which men often died. But when they were whipping some seaman they had another man standing by his side with a bucket of salt water, which he would throw into the open whip-wounds after each strike.

Oh, David thought—squirming as the salt touched the small cuts and scratches on his sides and arms—it must have been unbelievable. The pain from the salt water must have hurt worse than the whip.

He finished bathing. Then he took another bucketful and washed the cockpit out, and there was hunger.

It came with that speed. His mind was thinking of a sailor hanging on a rail with his back in ribbons and another man throwing salt water on the wounds and he dumped a bucket of water in the cockpit and he was hungry.

But now there was an awareness with it. This wasn't the hunger he'd felt before, which had to be filled right then— an emergency hunger. Now it was an ache, an emptiness that made him think as well as act. He found he could not separate his thoughts any longer.

He was hungry, and that made him think of food

and then of how much food he had, or didn't have, and that made him think again of where he was, how far from land he was, how far from help he was, and that made him think that there still was not a wind to drive him—didn't look like a wind coming either—and that made him circle back to the hunger.

So he wasn't just hungry. He was hungry with all his mind and body mixed in, hungry with the whole mix of his life caught in it.

"Which means I can't just eat," he said aloud. "All the other things have to be considered. . . ."

I am hungry, he thought, but I am hungry while I am becalmed over three hundred miles out to sea with no assistance available and one heck of a walk to a McDonald's.

I am hungry with a limited supply of food.

And, finally, I am hungry, but I cannot eat.

There it is, he thought. There is the thought I was working for but could not think. I am hungry, and there is some food in the boat, some limited food, but I cannot eat.

I must be very careful.

The knowledge tore at him that there was food down in the boat, some cans of food, cans of chili and fruit cocktail just lying around on the floor where they had been scattered by the storm, and he couldn't eat them.

Today was the first time in his life that he had

faced such a thing, and he knew also for the first time what it must be like to be poor, truly poor, and have hunger and not be able to do anything about it. Once he had seen a man in dirty clothes, a street man dressed in the dirt of the streets, walking down the aisle in a supermarket in Oxnard wearing an old field jacket, his eyes red and watering, his legs and feet shuffling along as he stared, just stared at the rows and rows of food that he could not have, could not buy, could not eat. When he'd seen the man David had been with his mother, and she had made some comment about a wino down on his luck, and David had agreed but now he knew it for what it was:

Hunger.

The man had wanted to eat, had been taken with hunger and the rows of food, but like David now could not eat.

It was then and was now a terrible thing. If David had been hungry and there was no food, he could have dealt with it more easily. But to be hungry and know there was some food, no matter how little, made the knowledge almost a form of torture, a teasing torture.

I could drink, he thought for a moment, and that would fill the emptiness and ease the hunger. But then he realized that he faced the same problem with water, fresh water. There was the tank built in to the front end of the boat for fresh water and he thought it held twenty gallons but he did not know how much water was in the tank. And as a matter of fact even if it were full, twenty gallons of water was not very much when he was not just thirsty but hungry and thirsty and three hundred miles out to sea with no wind and no help—not just thirsty but thirsty with all the rest of his life.

And that thought made him the more thirsty, made his lips dry and his tongue stick to the roof of his mouth.

All in seconds.

He shook his head and wiped his face with his hands. Small drops of sea water fell from his hair to the cockpit seat and he ran his hands through his hair to get more of the water out.

It was insane. Nothing had changed, really, but in just a few seconds he had gone from normal healthy thinking to being ravenously hungry and thirsty, his tongue stuck to the roof of his mouth, his stomach caving in toward his backbone—all without reason.

All, he thought, all in my mind.

Again, he shook his head. Well then—if he could think it he could unthink it. If it was all in his mind he could take it all out of his mind. And he did in only a few seconds more, and the feeling passed. He was still hungry and thirsty but it was controlled.

And there was work to do.

He pulled his shorts and jeans on but left his T-shirt off and tied it around the handrail line to air it out, although he put the lifejacket back on. On second thought he took his pants back off and tied them on the handrail as well. They were musty and stinky and he felt fresh now and it wasn't as if there were a lot of people around to see him romping about in his underwear and a lifejacket.

He had to finish putting the *Frog* back together and he had to take some kind of inventory and figure out just what he had.

Or didn't have.

10

He counted seven large, number 10, cans of food: two of chili, two of beef stew, two of vegetable soup, and one of fruit cocktail. There was also a bag of flour and another of sugar but they had both broken open and salt water had mixed and sloshed thoroughly in them, and he assumed the contents were ruined. He started to throw the bags out but thought better of it. Even with the salt water mixed in there might be some food value left in the flour and sugar.

That was it. No other food. And looking at the pitiful little pile on the table made it hard for David to stay cheerful.

The fresh water proved to be more encouraging. He located the filler cap under the front bunk cushions when he took all the cushions out and put them topside to dry in the sun. Strangely, in all his sailing with Owen, he had never filled the tank and didn't know where the cap was—Owen always had done the water when David came to the boat. Next to the cap was a label that said the tank held twenty-two gallons, instead of the twenty he had thought it might be, and when he opened and checked the water he found it to be almost full. He guessed close to twenty-one gallons. He pumped two cups and drank them immediately and found the water to be pure—although tasting still of the glass of the boat. No sea water had gotten in the tank in the roughness of the storm.

Somewhere he'd heard that normal usage of water was a gallon a day, and even at that rate he had enough for three weeks—twenty-one days. If he rationed it to half a gallon a day, which he thought he should, he was good for a month and a half; and if he went a month and a half without seeing anybody or getting rescued he'd be insane anyway. Or starved to death.

Probably starved, he thought, and the hunger pulsed up in him again.

He drank more water, three more cups—which seemed to help the hunger—and returned to work.

There were what seemed to be tons of equipment. Owen had always been one for having tools—what he called "gear."

"You've got to have lots of gear," he'd say. "Gear makes it all go."

Drawers of tools, winch handles, bins with anchors—not one but two of them, each with fifty feet of galvanized chain—and nylon rope for the anchors, called "rode," not rope, and he did not know why. Nor why they called the ropes that held the sails "sheets" and not ropes. Nor why they called the pulleys "blocks". Owen had never told him and he hadn't found a book to read on it yet. Under the left side of the forward bunk, along the edge of the water tank, there was a small but thick rod with a reel on it and heavy line and a canvas sack with small wrapped packets of fishing lures and hooks. There was also a strange, cone-shaped, extremely fine mesh net—a foot across at the mouth and tapering to a point, and perhaps eight feet long—that made no sense to David at all. Unless it was to hang things over the side to wash them or something . . .

Under the left couch bunk he found a deflated rubber dinghy and a plastic paddle, but there was no other survival gear, no flares or signaling devices, on the boat. Apparently Owen had never figured on being lost or having trouble at sea. He liked to sail mostly in coastal waters, up and down the coast to visit the small California towns, and probably just hadn't thought of being out very far.

There was one drawer full of small towels and washrags, another of silverware and knives—the one that had come loose and dumped everything on the floor during the storm—and everything, every single thing, was dripping. Water had gotten into all the drawers, in the storage compartments under all the cushions, into all the sail bags.

Everything was soaked.

As he removed and cleaned and checked the gear, he took the wetter things topside to dry in the sun, which was now beating down on the still boat like a broiler element. Soon the *Frog* was covered with cloth, cushions, drying sails, ropes, rags, and towels tied into all the lines that supported the mast—the shrouds and stays—and along the handrails.

David almost laughed out loud looking at her. Owen would have hated it, always liked the boat to be "tight and shipshape." David had her looking like a picture he'd seen of a Chinese junk in the harbor at Hong Kong, with several families living on the boat, drying their laundry in the rigging.

"Rag boat," he said to himself, standing in the cockpit under a cushion draped over the boom and dripping water. "Just an old rag boat."

The heat dried the thinner things rapidly, however, and within an hour the sails, towels, and two blankets were dry and folded and stored back in the boat in dry bags or drawers. The cushions, of four-inch-thick foam rubber, took longer. In the meantime he opened all the bins and aired them out. The inside of the *Frog* was baking hot; he opened the forward hatch wide, but it didn't help because there was still no air movement.

The day went rapidly as he worked. By late afternoon all the trash was cleaned up and in a plastic bag he'd found. He started to throw it over the side but stopped for two reasons—he thought it might attract sharks and he didn't want to do anything that attracted sharks, and he thought he might be able to use it.

Nothing was trash now, he thought. When he had nothing everything was valuable, and so he kept the sack of trash.

Just as evening came down he found a package wrapped tightly in a garbage sack, tied tightly so the water hadn't seeped inside. It felt heavy, book-like through the plastic. The inside of the cabin was getting dark, so he took the package topside to open it but stopped with his head out of the hatch opening.

The sunset, he thought—simply that thought. The sunset.

The sun seemed to be stopped just below the horizon, cutting gold bars through the water and slashing beams of light up, into the sky over his head.

For seconds, a full minute, he let the beauty of the sunset flood him, his brain blank, just pulling it in.

Then he sighed. No hunger then, no thirst, and for the time that the beauty was in him, no fear. Only the rolling sea and the bars of rich, cool light and the boat sliding up and down easily, as she was meant to, on the gentle swells. But in moments the feeling was gone and all the other facts were back. He was truly alone, sitting on a small boat far out in the Pacific Ocean.

Suddenly he remembered the plastic-wrapped package he was holding. He placed it on the cabin roof next to him. Standing on the top step and using the cabin top as a table, he carefully untied the wire twist-tie at the top and opened the bag.

Inside was a cloth-covered book, about ten by fourteen inches and just over an inch thick. He turned it to catch the light of the sunset, and across the top of the cover, written in black marker, were the words:

THE VOYAGE OF THE *FROG*

And beneath the title, in smaller letters:

Being the Compleat Log of the Good Boat *Frog*

Owen had kept a log—all this time he had kept a log and David had not known of it. It was getting dark now, but David opened the cover and held the first page up to the fading light. It was dated almost a year and a half before, written clearly in Owen's small, precise handwriting, and it told of sailing for a day alone over the deep trench that ran between the mainland of California and the island of Santa Rosa. There had been whales feeding on plankton and he had tried pulling his plankton cone net but with only partial success. Not enough to try a plankton burger, but enough for a taste.

Plankton.

That was the cone net under the forward bunk with the fishing line. It was a plankton net. David knew about plankton from biology—they were also called krill: millions of tiny, some almost microscopic, shrimp-like animals that filled the oceans of the world. He had seen pictures of them taken through a magnifying lens. They looked like watery bugs. Many creatures fed on them, including blue whales, the largest of all animals, with mouths like huge strainers filled with a mesh called baleen; the whales would take in massive gulps of seawater and krill, strain out the water and swallow the krill.

But he hadn't thought people could eat them. Plankton were so small. You couldn't clean them in any way, would just have to eat the whole thing. Tiny little legs and shells and all.

Which would be kind of like eating bugs . . .

He'd have to think about that one for a while. He was hungry, but he wasn't up for eating bugs yet. There were seven cans of food. It would be hard to get his mind past the little legs and shells and feelers and actually swallow a mouthful of krill. Of course there was the hunger, and his stomach was definitely moving toward his backbone, but still . . . bugs, he thought. Actually eating bugs.

Then there was the rod and reel. He could eat fish. The ocean was full of fish. All he had to do was catch a fish and cook it and eat it.

He tried to read more, but the light was almost all gone now; a soft darkness was coming over the sea and the boat and his thoughts. He had found three small, fat candles and a flashlight with dead batteries. There were some matches in a Ziplock plastic bag, and he lit one of the candles and put it on a small saucer on the table and sat on the couch— bumping down on the hard plywood because the cushions were still wet up topside—to look more at the log.

There were not entries for every day, only those days Owen had been on the boat. Most, virtually all, of the entries were just notations about sailing for the day, the direction of the wind, how long he had been out, what the day had been like.

> Sailed four hours in strait between mnlnd. & island.
> Wind NW at twenty knots. Beautiful sun.
> Caught N wind and sailed wing-and-wing for three hours. Clean run with no roll.

Clearly the entries were a personal record and not meant to be read by other people. David came upon a page that began:

> Brought Susan aboard for sail out to islands. We anchored in Fries Cove and made love. . . .

The entry went on in some detail about the two days in Fries Cove, diving for abalone and lobster, swimming nude, making love—part of Owen's private life. David felt strange reading it, as if he were prying somehow, but yet he couldn't stop reading it either.

Finally he closed the log abruptly and blew out the candle. In the darkness he couldn't read it and was safe from his own curiosity. With the lights out and the log closed he realized how tired he was, and still sore from the beating he'd taken. The quiet lapping of the water against the hull and the whuff-thump of the halyards bumping against the mast as the boat rocked made his eyelids weigh a ton and he leaned over on the plywood bench and fell into a deep sleep.

The oil tanker came about midnight.

11

He heard-felt a deep thrumming that seemed to come from the sea through the hull. It cut into his sleep until he opened one eye, closed it, shook his head and came more fully awake.

The sound was louder. Almost a rumble now, a waterborne thunder that actually made the hull vibrate when he put his hand against it. For part of a second the sound was so alien he could not place it. Then it came.

Engines! Ship engines. They had found him. He was saved!

Huge engines were driving a ship, still louder now

and closer, and he rolled off the bunk and jumped to the rear hatch to yell, to wave.

A gray wall was thundering toward the *Frog* in the moonlight—too close. A high gray wall of steel that was the side of an immense oil tanker rumbled toward him, a rolling white froth at its bow.

Too close! It didn't seem that the ship could miss. The thing was giant, filled the whole night horizon, filled the sky, filled the sea. Covered with lights it was like a city, a moving city of noise bearing down on him.

He slammed the rear hatch, ran back through the cabin, and pulled the front hatch into place. There was still no wind so he could not hope to sail, could not hope to move the boat.

He jumped back to the cockpit. Maybe if he held the tiller over he could turn the *Frog*. . . .

So fast. It all came so fast. Asleep one second, the tanker on him the next.

The noise was deafening—now a full-throated, throbbing roar that filled the water and air.

Flashing images. Some red paint and white numbers that seemed to tower over him. High, high and away, the glaring white lights of the bridge— he thought he could see small figures there, little people moving in the white light. Then it was on him.

On the *Frog*.

He wanted to close his eyes, wanted to make it all a dream but there was no time now to do anything more.

The bow of the tanker reared above him but did not collide. It slid sideways past, above him but past, and he thought that it could not be that big, could not be that huge and not hit the *Frog*.

The bow wave of the tanker hit him then, a large curl of water kicking sideways from the ship. Cushions that had still been up top, drapped on the handrails and boom, were knocked over the side into the water.

David grabbed the tiller and tried to keep the stern aimed at the side of the tanker, but without any forward movement she wouldn't steer, couldn't turn. The wave grabbed her, pushed her over until it seemed the mast and sail were skidding along the surface of the water. She was surfing on her side, surfing, and if the tip of the mast caught the water she'd flip over and down and fill and sink.

All in one motion she'd be gone. And he'd be gone. Caught in the giant screws of the tanker, churned to pieces.

Something came then, some instinct. In horror he watched the mast skid lower and still lower until he knew he had to do something, anything. He had been holding the tiller into his stomach in reflex, he now slammed it away, pushed it to the far side of the boat and held it, leaning until it seemed he was looking straight down into the black water.

And it worked.

When the tiller slammed over it caused the *Frog*'s stern to give a quick jerk sideways. This movement in turn pushed her bow slightly back up the wave that had forced her down. It was a whipping movement, an abrupt snap, and in a looping, swinging motion the *Frog* slipped back around and up and took the main force of the pressure wave from the tanker bow-on.

Some water splashed over the front, but not more than a few gallons, and it sluiced quickly off the sides. The *Frog* took it easily.

The tanker thundered past, slower than he would have wished, but faster than he thought such a huge ship could move.

People, he thought. There are people right there—right on the other side of that steel, there-are-people-right-there.

"Hey!" he yelled. "Hey-hey-hey-hey . . ." Until he could not control it and it became a near scream, but the rumble of the tanker's engines drowned out any chance his voice would carry.

For a full minute the tanker passed—so close, he thought, so close he could see the rivets in her hull and the water pumping out of exhaust holes on her side. So incredibly close that when he looked high up on the top edge of her side he could see a single light bulb swinging on the end of a wire.

People. Right there.

Right there.

"Hey!" he cupped his hands around his mouth and bellowed as loudly as he could. *"HEY!"*

But nobody came to the rail, nobody heard. The stern was coming now, roaring past, and the turbulence caused by the tanker's screws bounced the *Frog* this way and that, though not as severely as he expected.

And then it was gone.

The high stern seemed to lean back over him for a moment, a long moment, and the tanker was gone, moving rapidly away.

"Wait!" David screamed. "Don't go. Wait. Wait now, somebody look back and wait."

He could see lights on the bridge from the rear, was certain now that he could see people, small people moving in the lights, but there was no indication anybody saw anything. No reaction.

How could they miss seeing him? The sails were still up, were catching the moonlight and must be visible for miles as a white triangle against the ocean. How could they not see them?

No flares. If only he had some flares. How was it possible that Owen had not put flares or some emergency light aboard?

Light. He needed some light.

The boat battery was dead, and the batteries in the only flashlight he'd found. The candle. That was it—his only light. The candle.

He scrambled below. In the violence of motion from the tanker's bow wave the candle and matches that had been on the table had been thrown off. Frantically he fell to his hands and knees and felt around beneath the table in the darkness, sweeping back and forth.

There. His fingers hit the candle and it rolled. He grabbed for it, missed, grabbed again and caught it. Then matches. The book of matches had skidded further, near the mast, and he found them only when he'd wasted moments crawling under the table to its other side.

He forgot himself and jumped for the rear hatch so fast he hit his head on the table top.

The tanker was still near, but moving away rapidly. He fumbled and dropped two matches before he struck one and held it to the wick of the candle. It lit immediately, sputtered once when he breathed on the new flame, caught and flared up.

He held it up, waved it carefully back and forth in a wide arc, left to right and back again. The movement made the flame flicker but it didn't go out. He tried a wider arc, stepping sideways from one side of the cockpit to the other, moving the candle slowly over his head and down.

The tanker kept moving. Away. There was no sign from the ship that they had seen the light.

"Please," he whispered aloud. "Please. See this. See the light. See the candle. Please."

He waved it wider and wider and the movement blew it out. With shaking hands he lighted it, waved it again.

Waved it and waved it until the lights, the bright lights of the tanker, had drawn together in the distance until they were only a blob of yellow on the horizon.

Waved the candle until the lights of the tanker were completely gone over the edge of the earth, gone from his life and his eyes forever, and still he waved.

Slowly, silently waved the candle.

In the night he knew layers of hate.

When David finally knew that the tanker had not seen him—that the tanker had almost hit him and still nobody had seen him, nobody had seen his light—he began to hate.

Not just to feel anger, but to know the yellow-red cut-edge of hate. He hated first the tanker, for almost killing him, for almost running him down. It was a beast, some huge beast of a killer that had nearly taken him down into the dark places, and he hated it, hated it with all the vicious anger and hatred he could make in his mind.

Somehow hating the ship made it easier to be angrier and hate other things. He hated whoever was

steering that tanker. A complete idiot, he thought—
how could such a complete idiot, such a damn fool
steer that giant ship? Didn't he look out over the bow
once in a while? Worse, he was probably sleeping up
there, just sleeping and not paying any attention to
where he was going. Miserable person. A really miserable damn fool of a human being . . .

And what about the radar operator? He must have
seen the *Frog* on his radar scope, right there in front
of the ship. David had seen tankers on television.
They were all equipped with the latest equipment,
and Owen had told him once that they kept the
radars on big ships going all the time, even in good
weather, because they showed other ships coming a
long way off. So how could someone not have seen
the *Frog* on that scope?

David moved like a drugged robot. The cushions
were floating all around the boat in the moonlight
and he fished them out. The ones that had drifted
too far he reached with the small paddle for the
rubber dinghy. He spread them once more along the
top of the cabin and in the rear of the cockpit, cursing
all the while.

Hate was like a fuel that drove him, kept him
stumbling around in the darkness, picking up this
and that inside the boat, slamming it down, swearing
and hating, always hating.

He hated the storm that had driven him out to

sea and hurt him, hated the wind that didn't come so he could sail home, hated things he should have loved, hated Owen for dying, hated his parents for having him, and, finally, hated himself.

Sitting at the table in the darkness, the moonlight slatting into the cabin through the small windows in bars of pale white, he hated himself more than all the rest. Hated his stupidity for sailing so far out before the storm took him. It was insane to do that, just stupid and insane. Hated himself for learning to sail, for wanting to sail. Why couldn't he just want to have a normal life on shore? Why did he have to be so stupid and want to sail and want to learn from Owen? And in the end, in the steaming little pit of hatred and poison, he found himself, he found the David he needed.

His foot brushed the log where it had fallen in all the motion and he picked it up and put it on the table.

He hated the log. The hatred, he thought, almost coldly—the hatred was total. It was the middle of the night and he didn't want to sleep, didn't want to be awake, didn't want to be or not be—only wanted to hate. Just sit in the dark and hate everything.

He realized that he was grinding his jaws together so hard his back teeth and the muscles in his cheeks were starting to ache.

He opened the log. Moonlight fell on the pages and he turned them until he came to a blank one. He lit the stub of candle in the saucer where he'd put it when he came back into the cabin.

In the drawer beneath the sink there were three pencils and he took one out and wrote in the log:

Date unknown, probably June 4th or 5th. No wind.
Near collision with an oil tanker which didn't stop.
I am hate.

And when he saw it written, saw it spelled out, he realized how ridiculous it was to think hate, live hate, be hate. It accomplished nothing. Hatred just made more hatred—and when you were done with it nothing had been gained. You just got hate. He sighed in the candlelight and erased the last sentence. He wrote:

I am alone.

And seeing what he'd written had the same effect as before, brought the words home to him. He was truly on his own, would have to make things work. Up to now he had been thinking only in temporary terms. If he could make another day, another few hours, he thought, they would find him, would come for him. It was just a matter of keeping things going. But it might not be that way. They might not find him. He might be weeks getting back, or might never get back—it was up to him. Up to just David, and no other person could be counted on. He couldn't say "Time out" and have it all stop. This is it, he thought, seeing it written—I am alone. And this isn't a temporary situation—or might not be. I'm all I've got.

He closed the log, blew out the candle and lay back on the hard plywood with a lifejacket for a pillow. One of the plastic snaps stuck in his ear and he rolled the jacket to make it more comfortable.

Sleep came slowly, fought against the last bit of anger and self pity and finally won, and David closed his eyes.

Just me, he thought, sliding deep—it's all on me.

Sun broiling down.

The inside of the cabin was unbelievably hot. He opened his eyes, sat up on the bench and rolled to his feet, his head out the top of the rear hatch.

The sun was high overhead. Midday, he thought, judging it to be almost exactly between the west and east horizons. I slept through the morning and into the middle of the day.

The excitement and disappointment of the night had left him hammered down with tiredness, and in spite of the hardness of the bench without the cushion he had slept well, overslept as a matter of fact, and he felt rested.

Still no wind.

He looked quickly at the sea, saw that the swells were still rolling toward the *Frog* in long, oily moves, and turned away. Then he remembered the night before, remembered that he was different now, had vowed to be different.

He looked again at the swells, studied them. With the back of his hand he wiped his mouth to get the night taste out. . . .

They weren't the same.

The swells at first seemed to be the same as the day before, but when he looked more closely he could tell the difference. They were a little faster, more abrupt, with here and there less than a smooth curve at the top, almost a breaking point. A kind of roughness, or at least the feeling of roughness coming.

So, he thought—it's different, but what does it mean?

A change.

It must mean a change coming.

And the way it was now, any change would be a good one. Dead calm, the sky a flat-copper blue and the heat so thick inside the boat that it was hard to get breath down—any change would be welcome.

Would mean wind. A change could mean some wind coming.

He returned to the sink and drank four cups of water, sloshing it through his teeth before swallowing. Almost as good as brushing, he thought.

Hunger was triggered by the water but not as bad as before. He thought momentarily about eating, then decided to eat in the evenings. Only water in the mornings, food at night.

He would get a ritual going. There would be a water time and a food time, a schedule for each day there was no wind. A work time, he thought, there had to be a work time each day when he could finish getting the boat back into shape, get it ready for when the wind came again. There would be a work time and a food time and a water time and . . .

There was something else there, in his mind, but he couldn't pin it down at first. Something else he should do with each day. A thing . . .

A learning time. Another thought from the night before, one that must have come while he was sleeping. He had to know more or he wouldn't make it. He should try to learn each day. It was like Owen had said—he wanted to know everything. David felt that now, felt that he had to know things, know all things, but there wasn't a way to learn on the boat, not a way to study and gain knowledge. There were no books, no radio.

Just me, he thought—just me. He looked at the sea again, the sky, letting his mind roll. Could I study myself? Can it be done? Can a person study his own brain? He shook his head, cleared the thoughts, and without thinking put a hand on one of the cushions, then another, and almost cheered. They were dry. The sun had baked even the last dampness out of them.

One by one he took them down and brought them inside the cabin. It had seemed so empty with the bare plywood bunks and seats, hollow and echoing. The cushions filled it out, made it more livable, more comfortable.

He worked the rest of the afternoon doing the small things. The sails were dry and he bagged them all except the working jib and mainsail which he left up, hanging like limp rags waiting for wind.

Always waiting for wind.

And then it was done, all done. He could find nothing more to do now. Everything was put away, in good shape. He had inventoried all that he had, or didn't have.

It was all finished. He couldn't believe it, somehow. Trash bagged, cleaning done—he had even wiped the small countertop next to the sink with a towel dampened in salt water—there wasn't a single thing left to do.

Except wait.

13

Another night and another full day and yet another evening passed, dragged, pulled along so slowly that it was maddening.

Water in the morning. Four plastic cups. He figured that as close to a quart. Four more cups at night. Two quarts equalled half a gallon. His daily ration. Hot as it became he didn't feel thirsty on half a gallon a day except for the first night.

That first evening after the tanker nearly hit him he opened one can of beef stew for food and ate it cold. He didn't want to waste any of the small amount of alcohol for the stove on something that didn't need cooking. As soon as he took a bite the hunger became uncontrollable, and he wolfed down half the can before he could stop. It was viciously salty and he had to drink water as soon as he put the plastic spoon down; then he forced himself to cover the can with a piece of plastic wrap and save the other half for tomorrow.

He tried fishing the next day. The little plastic tackle case had a small variety of silver spoons and some feathered lures, and he tried them all. The rod and reel were strung with a heavy line and thin steel cable for a leader. No matter the lure, fishing shallow or deep, jiggling or letting it hang still, it didn't matter—nothing bit. It was as if the ocean were completely empty of fish. He fished for five hours without a bite, through the day and up to the food time for the second day after the tanker and never got a single indication there was a chance of catching anything, big or little. He would even have welcomed the shark. But nothing came.

Which didn't help his frustration.

He then unwrapped the second half of the stew. But it had been sitting in the sink all day in the heat and smelled funny. He ate it anyway and within half an hour was sick to his stomach and had to sit on the chamber pot bucket kept in the small compartment beneath the front bunk. The sickness didn't last long, but kept him doubled over for an hour or so and left him weak enough to want to sleep again—and that ended another day.

Another dead day.

The learning experiment wasn't successful either. In complete boredom the next day he tied a large towel beneath the boom and over to the handrails on either side to make an awning and sat in the shade. The inside of the cabin was so hot it was unlivable.

He thought he'd sit and think and try to remember things he must have learned that were still in his mind. The idea was sound but he couldn't make it work. He knew he had read stories about the sea, knew that Owen had told him many things, knew that he had learned some from watching television and movies, but all that came to him was the scene from *Jaws* in which the shark was trying to eat the back end of the boat—which Owen had told him was complete nonsense—and the beginning of Lincoln's Gettysburg address.

"Four score and seven years ago our fathers brought forth on this continent a new nation . . ."

Which was nice except it didn't help him in his particular situation. Of course, once *Jaws* and Lincoln were in his head he couldn't get them out, and he sat for an hour thinking of different scenes from the movie and trying to remember everything he could about Lincoln—which wasn't much. And that bothered him because he didn't think it was quite right that he should know more about a funky movie about a mechanical shark than about a president, so he got into trying to summon up more about Lincoln than *Jaws*, and when it was finally done—he figured in the end they were about even because he remembered the mole on Lincoln's cheek and thought that was a pretty good detail—he had frittered away most of the afternoon without learning anything and he leaned back and saw the plane.

It was a high jet, leaving a white contrail, heading from east to west, right over the top of him, and for a second his heart jumped. There were people there, inside that little speck of aluminum, just as there had been people in the tanker, people that close. Then he realized it didn't matter. If all he could see of the huge plane was a tiny speck barreling along in front of the white line no one in the plane could possibly see him. Even if they were looking. Which they probably weren't. And even if they looked and saw him somehow it would just be a sailboat. . . . Without flares or some way to attract attention it didn't matter if anybody saw him or not. He looked again at the plane. The people were probably sitting there and the flight attendants were bringing them food and cold pop, probably lots of cold pop and hot food in those little trays with more cold pop whenever they wanted it, with lots of ice. Probably on their way to

Hawaii and they could probably just eat or drink cold drinks whenever they wanted to. . . .

"Ahh . . ." He swore. It was enough. The situation was bad enough without making it worse by torturing himself. He would think himself into another layer of hate.

And somehow evening came again and he went into the cabin—which cooled instantly and felt wonderful once the sun went down because the seawater kept the hull cool—to eat and sleep. He ate half a can of chili and put the rest in the small ice chest beneath the steps. It wasn't cold, because he had no ice, but it felt a little cooler to his touch than the air. He hoped the chili would keep.

He fell asleep in the captain's bunk without a cover, his head resting again on a lifejacket, completely sick of the day, his mind filled with pictures of a white shark and Lincoln and a bunch of people on a plane drinking cold pop and eating great plates of steaming food.

Disgusting.

Something had awakened him and he lay listening, his senses keyed and alert, the memory of the tanker fresh in his mind.

Almost totally dark. A sliver of a moon made some light but very little of it came into the darkened cabin. He held his breath and listened but heard nothing—no engines, no thumps on the hull. No danger. Then it came, a gentle, almost puffing whispering sound.

"Whuff-whuff . . ."

The mainsail luffing.

Wind.

He rolled out of the bunk, put his head out of the cabin top. In the faint light the sea seemed the same, swells sliding under him, the boat moving easily on them. Then he felt it.

"Whuff-whuff."

A faint breeze, a touch on his cheek, just enough to move the ends of his hair, the sail moving back and forth gently. Wind.

Oh yes, he thought, sweet wind, fine wind, wind wind wind . . .

He jumped into the cockpit and untied the towel which was still stretched from the boom to make an awning. He threw the towel into the cabin, then slammed the tiller over to the side and held it with his leg while he pulled in on the main sheet and cleated it off. Then he tighted the jib a bit but left it loose and billowing to catch the light air.

The movement of the helm pulled the bow over slowly, ever so slowly until it was pointed dead east—ninety degrees on the compass numbers glowing in the darkness—and now the sails filled like two ghost wings against the sky and the *Frog* started to move.

He found after a bit of experimentation that he couldn't point her very high, toward the direction of the wind, which was almost straight out of the north, because in such a light wind she would just stop. But if he sailed across the wind, let the sails fill on a soft broad reach, she would keep moving—and soon he heard the wake burbling as she gained speed, held three knots, moved almost to four, then back to three and a half.

Sailing. Oh yes, he thought again, oh yes, wind, come and take me home. She was sailing dead east and making three and a half knots and that way lay the land. That way lay California. That way lay home.

Take me home, wind, take me home, wind. . . .

Home wind.

Homewind.

14

The wind freshened throughout the night, gradually increasing until the *Frog* was boiling happily along at a steady four and a half knots. David sailed all night, held her off the wind and let the sails fill and draw well. After sitting for days waiting for wind, after the frustration and boredom, it seemed that the *Frog* had taken life, was flying across the sea and he hated to stop even to go to the bathroom. Once he tied the rudder off with a piece of cord so he could go below and get a drink of water but as soon as he drank he returned to the cockpit.

He kept sailing, holding her off the wind, gaining speed a little each hour, driving her, letting her ride the wind until he saw a sliver of light ahead, the sun coming up in the east and just as the sun broke out, the top curve of gold brilliance shafting across the water, he heard a sound, a high-pitched squeaking sound and the splashing of water and a killer whale rose right next to him in the water.

His heart almost stopped.

The whale was enormous, rising so that its front half was totally clear of the water, towering over him, looking down on him, studying him. The black skin glistened with water, the white markings so defined they looked painted by an artist. High on the side the whale's right eye stared at him, rotating, taking in everything in the cockpit. The eye looked intelligent, almost human.

David couldn't cry out, couldn't think, couldn't do anything. And before he could breathe again, another whale rose, then another and still another until four of them surrounded the cockpit, moving with the boat in tandem, looking down on David sitting beneath them.

They were beautiful and frightening, stunningly frightening at the same time. He felt lost, empty, gone—if they wanted they could reach over and take him, just pluck him out of the boat any time.

I could run below, he thought. Let the tiller go and hide below. But they could simply run into the hull and batter a hole in it if they wanted him.

He held course, wished for more wind, wished

for speed, but knew that even on her best day with the best wind he could not outrun them. Somewhere he'd heard that they could swim twenty to thirty knots an hour. They could circle him at the fastest speed he could hope to make, just loop around him with ease. Play with him.

They started making sounds. High-pitched squeaking sounds with clicks at odd intervals over the top of him, back and forth. One would make the sound, another would answer, then the third one picked it up, and finally the fourth, and it would start over.

They're talking about me, he thought. No. They're talking me over—talking about what to do with me. Like I was a toy. Or something to eat. Well. Well, I'm not. Not yet.

"I'm David Alspeth," he said aloud, directing his words to the whale nearest on the left. The eye glittered straight into his. "I don't mean any harm. I only want to sail home."

He felt silly, speaking to them, but then thought they might feel silly speaking over him as well. There was no outward indication that his voice meant anything to them. The one nearest him on the left—he felt it must be the leader but had no idea why—moved momentarily closer to him, leaned over him, but before David could react or jump into the cabin the whale moved away again, made three more squeaks and a click and lowered back into the water.

The other whales did the same, their huge dorsal fins flopping over to the side, curving up out of the water as they swam next to the *Frog*, almost in formation with her. They would move away a bit, then swim in closer and closer until more than once they bumped the hull, not hard, but bumped it so the *Frog* moved sideways a bit with each nudge. Then out, swim, and in close, out and in for miles.

The whales stayed with him well into the morning, nearly to midday, but he did not feel them as a threat. It was more like the dolphins. David knew that sometimes dolphins would run ahead of a boat, stay just beneath the bow, and play with the boat as it sailed and he felt the killer whales were playing with him now.

They were not enemies. They could have taken him easily if they had wanted to attack him. Lord, he thought, watching one swim close and away—Lord, it is longer than the boat, bigger than the boat, my home, all that I am, and it is bigger. A living animal bigger than all that I am. Lord. And he suddenly remembered a prayer he had seen on a plaque for sale in the store at the marina.

"Lord," he said the prayer aloud. "Your sea is so large and my boat is so small—have mercy." Even Your whales, he thought, even Your whales are bigger than my boat. Have mercy.

In the end he decided they were friends: coursing next to him with their great beauty for hours, holding their speed down to stay with him as he worked at sailing the *Frog* east, always east, running across the steady wind. And finally, when they turned and headed north, dead into the wind where he could not follow, he felt a sadness at their going, their leaving him.

He waved, watching the whales—he had to think to remember they were called a pod—watching them turn as if on command and cut north, picking up speed and slipping through the short waves the wind was now causing; he waved at them and wished they were not going, wished they were staying with him to run across this wonderful wind.

Everything was different now. There was good wind, fresh enough so he could point the *Frog* up a bit and run slightly north of east and still hold good speed. He wasn't sure where he was, had actually no idea where he could possibly be with any exactness but he figured California had to be almost straight east and that he would have to hit somewhere along the coast if he kept going. He thought maybe down the coast a bit, maybe straight out from Los Angeles, because the storm had blown him south a bit as well as out to sea.

But it didn't matter now. He marveled at how his situation could change so much just because there was a wind. Such a little thing and it changed his whole life. One minute everything was awful and looked terrible and then a little wind could come and flop everything over.

It was as if he suddenly owned the world—he and the *Frog* owned the ocean, owned all of the ocean and the world was mostly ocean. He could go anywhere. With wind he could go anywhere, see anything, be anything. With wind he could move with the whales, with wind everything was possible.

He thought he should feel sleepy after sailing all night, but the daylight seemed to drive away sleep and his body hummed with the boat and wind and sea. He tied the helm off again, more loosely this time so she would come up into the wind. But it would take a long time and that gave him a few moments to step below and drink four cups of water. Then he stretched and touched his toes to take away the night stiffness and went to the bathroom.

When he climbed again out of the cabin top he saw that she was starting to swing up a bit more. He took his T-shirt off and stood to the helm, not sitting but standing with the tiller handle against his leg, the boat heeled over at a mild angle. He tuned the sails to tighten the curve, stood again with his hip cocked, feeling the boat vibrate through the wood of the tiller into his hand and against his hipbone, and sailed.

It was a joy. The sun was already hot and the wind solid and growing a bit each hour and he got the *Frog* up to five knots and held it until the sun was straight overhead. In the heat of being becalmed he had burned and begun to tan, and now with the wind and the spray of a night and half a day his body had become weathered and brown-gold. His hair was already bleaching out to a lighter blond that would become white and his eyes were lined at the corners from squinting.

In the afternoon he saw clouds coming from his back, from the northwest, low clouds moving fast, and the wind stiffened again, pushing the *Frog* over to a more severe heeling angle though she still sailed well, and for the first time he thought of himself and the *Frog* as "we."

"Well," he said aloud to her—not to himself but to the boat, "I guess we should reef sail if the wind is going to keep getting stronger."

And he meant we—he could no longer draw a line where he ended and the *Frog* began. He looked down at his bare feet, planted firmly on the floor of the cockpit, the vibration, the hum, the life of the *Frog* coming up through them into his legs, and he knew it would be we from now on. They were together, a thing of the sea and the wind and man all joined in a single dance.

To sail.

To turn the force of the wind and sea, the force of the earth and a person, into a dance across the water.

He wished he could sing and actually tried a verse but his voice was so bad it didn't feel right. If I were a dolphin, he thought suddenly, if I were a dolphin I would be the kind that swims just in front of the boat and leaps out of the water and spirals.

I would be a dolphin that dances.

He let the helm go and the *Frog* nosed up into the wind and lost her heel instantly. The sails started luffing, slapping in a breeze that wasn't as strong as he'd thought while he was sailing but he decided to reef anyway.

The process wasn't too complicated. He'd seen Owen do it twice, maybe three times. The idea was to reduce the area of the mainsail so it wouldn't catch so much wind. It was done by rotating the boom and wrapping the sail around it, like a rolled up window shade, until it was reduced enough so the wind couldn't blow the boat over.

The boom was mounted to the mast on a gear knuckle with a worm gear and all that was required was to loosen the main halyard and use a crank handle for the winch to roll the boom.

It took him a moment to find the crank in the drawer beneath the sink and only a few minutes to roll the boom and bring the mainsail to about three quarters of its normal size. In that time the wind picked up, suddenly clouds covered the horizon, and some small ones gathered directly overhead.

He put the crank away, held the helm over to back her around a bit until the sails filled and she was moving once more. The sails didn't pull as well but the boat still made four knots and he had more control. She didn't heel as much when the wind gusted, which it did now with some frequency, and he sailed until close to dark—slamming now through the waves, spray hitting him when the bow plowed into a large one—sailed until he couldn't take it anymore. He'd been up for he guessed nineteen or twenty hours without rest or food, and the tiredness soaked into him.

He let her come into the wind, went below and slipped his T-shirt and windbreaker on. There was a coolness to the evening air that made him shiver. The rest of the chili was still in the ice chest and he ate it cold—it didn't smell bad, or any worse than chili always smelled—working around the yellow hunks of fat. Hungry as he was he couldn't bring himself to eat them, and he pitched them over the side.

15

Movement awakened him, but not with any urgency. The *Frog* was rolling a bit more and had nearly dumped him out of the bunk. When his eyes slid open, his ears began to work as well, and he heard the wind whistling in the rigging and halyards and the sails crackling as they luffed; he realized that there were some waves making up. That's how he thought it. Not as he would have a week before, as somebody in a parking lot in Ventura, California, who would think of waves growing larger. He thought, there are waves making up, and that was a nautical way to think, and he did not know why he'd think that way now but he did. He sat up in the bunk and stood to put his head out the cabin top.

It was absolutely pitch dark. Clouds had come to cover the sliver moon and stars, and even the sails, so white and usually easy to see, were practically invisible.

The wind was strong, but not wild. Just a good, strong, steady force. He drank more water, rinsing his mouth, put the lifejacket on, and backed the boat around to catch the breeze.

She had been waiting for it. The jib fairly popped with energy, filled and pulled her out and away. The main, still reefed, he tightened a bit to match the jib and the *Frog* seemed to leap ahead. She ran into the first wave like a truck hitting a wall. The hull gave a resounding *thump* and she seemed nearly to stop. Then the wind drove her again and she hit the next wave and nearly stopped again.

It was like riding a roller coaster while somebody every twenty seconds hits the front end with a giant sledgehammer. Each time the boat drove into a wave, water shot back across her top in a dashing spray that almost knocked him over. He hung onto the high-side lifeline with one hand, the tiller with the other, and braced himself tightly into the cockpit. But still, when the *Frog* slammed into the next wave and the water hit him, he had trouble keeping his balance.

By the tenth wave he knew they couldn't do it.

He had been holding straight east trying to head back to what he figured should be Los Angeles or maybe a bit south of that. But it was impossible. The slamming of the sea had already jarred open the drawers beneath the sink—and he hadn't really started. If he tried to hold course and continue to take the waves nearly head on he wasn't sure the boat could handle it. The noise was deafening.

He let her fall off the wind, so that she was pointing south of straight east. Down to a hundred, then a hundred and twenty degrees and finally—when she was pointing at close to one thirty on the glowing compass dial and moving more with the waves than quartering against them—she settled down.

The change was astounding. It was like a different ocean. The noise virtually disappeared, the slamming stopped, and the *Frog* surfed down the long swells and waves so fast she sometimes showed close to ten knots on the speed indicator.

"Now this is something," he said to her, holding fast to the tiller as it fairly sang with speed-vibration. "This is really something."

Soon he was keeping to a steady eight knots, surging to nine and ten when she surfed and slid down the waves. He laughed with the speed, reveled in it, roared with it—the *Frog* like a train barreling down a mountain.

He had held her that way for two hours, then

another half an hour, when he sensed the danger.

Later he would try to remember what he knew, what he felt. It was perhaps a change in the wind's sound, or a change in the pattern of the sound of the sea that first warned him.

A second later he heard an actual hissing rumble that at first meant nothing to him. Then he looked ahead of her, squinting against the darkness and saw, or thought he saw, or felt that he thought he saw, a white line stretching horizontally.

Which made as little sense as the rumble until he put the two together and realized that what he was seeing, thought he was seeing, was surf.

And close. Breaking right in front of him.

He was about to run up on a beach!

He slammed the tiller over just as he felt the surf grab the boat and begin to carry them into the fatal run to shore. The waves were huge and he could hear them well now, thundering against a beach he still could not see. His life and the life of the *Frog* were measured in seconds. Her nose came around, past the beach, aiming more and more out to sea.

She hit then, the keel-centerboard bumping with a sickening feeling that shuddered all through him, a lurching, dead feeling. But before she could strike hard and be driven down, the nose came back through the wind and the sails filled. He released the right jib sheet, frantically pulled in the left, felt the sail fill and begin to draw, pulling, pulling the *Frog* away from shore.

Another bump, worse than the first, the surf crashing all around him and suddenly, impossibly, she was free and reaching again, the surf-sound diminishing.

Alive.

And land. He had found land.

The elation held for several moments. Then he realized that if he were within a hundred miles of Los Angeles or even further down near San Diego, the sky would be glowing, the whole world would be light.

He had found land, but it was dark. There wasn't a sign of civilization.

Where was he?

16

He sailed west slowly for two hours, holding about four knots, which, he figured, put him a good two miles away from the shore, then he let her come up into the wind and drift to a stop. He could continue to sail, but to move blind in the dark this close to an unknown shore would be madness. If something went wrong he could be driven up on the rocks and sunk. If there were any rocks. He could barely see his hand in front of his face. The wind took the *Frog* backward, but with the sails loose and slatting she moved so slowly that she was effectively still.

He went below in the darkness, drank two glasses of water to celebrate finding land, then went back up to the cockpit to sit and wait for dawn. Confusion ruled him. He had at least thought that he'd hit California. This was nothing. He must have drifted farther south than he thought possible. A current must have carried him, even when he was becalmed. Some crazy current. He was at land, but he was nowhere.

A light sleep took him, a dozing, and it seemed that as soon as his eyes closed he opened them to see a graying in the clouds to the east and in another half hour he could see the land.

It was a low, gray sand mass that stretched from north to south before him, and as the light rapidly grew better—though the clouds kept the sun from actually shining—he could see that it was a desert coast. His heart sank. There were low bluffs, rock and sand and dunes that dimmed away out of sight, but no sign of any human habitation.

"Ahhh . . ." he hissed to himself. He'd thought that if he could get back to land it would be over. Get back to soil and there would be people and he could tie her up to a dock in a marina and call his parents and they would come to him and bring him food. A hamburger and a malt, a cold malt and fries—two hamburgers and two malts and fries— and he would sit and eat and tell everybody about the storm and the killer whales. . . .

When he saw land, he'd thought, he would know it was over.

And now he saw land, almost ran up on it, and there was nothing. Not a single mark of any kind of man.

Desert. Bleak and dry and sandy with rock ridges.

Baja. He was at Baja.

The sun was full up now and the light good. To the south the line of sand and surf stretched as far as he could see with no break. But to the north, two miles up—he stood to see it—there was a break in the surf line almost half a mile long. It might be some kind of harbor or bay.

It was north of where he could point the *Frog* and move against the wind, so he backed her around and tacked out to sea, holding her against the slamming waves as steadily as he could until the break in the coast was slightly to the rear. Then he brought her around and headed in, aiming for the center of the break in the surf line, which he could now see was close to a mile wide.

The wind had picked up a bit of morning strength and the *Frog* greased along well. He stood at the tiller to see better and soon he was coming through the opening. Straight ahead he could see more beach, about a mile away, but to the left and northward there was a large bay that must have stretched close to three miles. It was surrounded by low sand hills—he could see some cactus now that he was closer to land, and some kind of short, spiny plant that he had seen in pictures but couldn't name—and was so perfectly sheltered that down low the water was protected from the wind. It was as smooth as a small lake, though the sails were up high enough to catch some breeze. When he was fairly close to shore he tacked left and started up the bay and within minutes they were free of any sea swell or wave action. The *Frog* glided gently, and slower, as the hills grew higher and blocked more and more of the north wind. David held her close along the west shore, looking for any sign of man.

There was nothing. Not a track, not a board, nothing. Just empty sand and rocks. Nothing green except the cactus and spiny plants. Blue water washing up to gray sand and nothing else.

He was, suddenly, completely exhausted. He had sailed all of one night and a day and most of the next night, taking energy from the wind, with only three or four hours of sleep. There was no help here for him, that was clear now, but it was a perfect anchorage and he decided to anchor and spend a day resting before deciding what to do next.

He moved in closer to shore, skidding along. Something in him said anchor close to shore, maybe even swim ashore. But the centerboard twice rubbed on the bottom lightly, so he took her back out a bit to deeper water until he had covered most of the bay and still found no sign of civilization.

He had anchored with Owen, once in a crowded small bay with other boats, where it was difficult because they had to put out two anchors to keep from swinging around and hitting other boats. The second time they had been the only boat in a harbor at Santa Cruz Island and Owen had anchored only from the bow.

"It's the best way," he had told David. "She can move with any change in the wind, swing around to keep her nose into it. You just need room."

Well, David thought, looking at the empty water, I've got plenty of room. . . .

He turned her into the middle of the bay and let her come up into the wind and stop. The *Frog* rode without moving on the still water, the sails flapping slowly in the breeze.

The anchors were wrapped and coiled neatly beneath the captain's bunk and he took the larger of them—a spade-type anchor with fifty feet of galvanized chain and two hundred feet of nylon rope—up to the bow.

Carefully, so the chain wouldn't rub on the boat and mar the finish—Owen had always worried about the finish and without really meaning to David found himself looking for new scratches or scrubs—he lowered the anchor. The water was surprisingly shallow, perhaps only forty or fifty feet, and when the anchor was on the bottom he paid the rope out as the *Frog* moved slowly, so slowly backward in the light air. Twice he caught himself dozing off and snapped awake.

Finally he figured that he had out nearly a hundred feet of rope, plus the chain, and that the anchor was properly digging into the bottom. Owen had said that the *Frog* needed a hundred feet to be securely anchored if there were mild waves and not too heavy a wind, and in this sheltered, smooth water and gentle breeze she would stay.

He tied the rope to a cleat at the bow and moved back to the cockpit. It took just a few minutes to drop the sails and wrap them. He coiled the jib on itself and let it lie—ready to use if needed rapidly. The mainsail he wrapped around the boom and tied with three short pieces of cord.

The morning sun was high now, coming to mid-day and getting wildly hot. He could not sleep inside the cabin—he'd bake. He rigged the towel to the boom to act as a sunshade and brought a bunk cushion up. After four cups of water he lay back on the cushion in the shade of the towel and closed his eyes.

He had, somehow, never felt so secure in his life and was asleep, into deep sleep, within thirty seconds.

17

"Ahhhhwwwkkk!"

David rolled to his knees in the bottom of the cockpit and fought the urge to vomit. The stink was so putrid, so vile—some kind of rotten fish odor mixed with hot breath and sticky seawater—he couldn't stand it: a thick stink, a rotten-rich-thick stink that filled every corner of his sleep and awakened him and drove him to his knees before his eyes were even open.

He dry heaved three times, controlled it, and rose to his feet, rubbing his eyes to see what had happened. There was something sticky in his hair and down the back of his neck, and he wiped it off gingerly. When it stuck to his fingers he wiped them on the towel awning.

The bay was alive with whales.

He had slept the afternoon away and it was getting close to dusk, although there was still plenty of sun showing over the water and hills to the west, and all around him, all around the boat in the bay, were whales.

Huge whales. Great whales. Wonderful whales.

Before he could take in the whole scene, an enormous back rolled out of the water near the *Frog* and a whale blew, a mighty vaporous cloud of breath and spray as its lungs expelled air and David caught the same odor that had covered him while he slept. A whale must have surfaced right next to the *Frog* and blown on him.

Talk about bad breath! Rotten krill, shrimp, plankton, small fish—they ate it all—mixed with gallons of . . . what? Snot? God. Maybe that's what was in his hair. Maybe the whale that blew on him had a cold. Yuuckkkk. He grabbed the towel and scrubbed his hair and neck, then rinsed the towel over the side.

He could not be sure of the kind of whale because he didn't know enough to identify them, but he thought they might be blues, and they literally almost filled the bay. A whole pod of them must have come in while he slept: some small—he saw several with calves—and some large and some so immense they seemed to fill the sea, fill the world, and they were all around him.

One rose out of the water, his head high in the air, then fell over with a mighty, booming splash and as if on signal another rose and yet another until whales were rising and falling all around him.

A gigantic set of flukes came out of the water not fifty feet away and splashed down so hard the water sprayed all over David and left half an inch to drain out of the cockpit well. Beyond the first one another set of flukes rose, waved, then crashed down and was followed immediately by two more whales that raised their front halves out of the water and fell over. . . .

All for me, David thought. Alone here in the bay the whales are for me.

And for the *Frog*.

See them, *Frog*? See them dance for us? He wished intensely that he had somebody to share it with and that wish made him think of his parents and Owen and in turn made him think of them, miss them, so that it almost stopped his breath. He forced his mind back to the whales.

He could not be sure how many there were because some went down while others came up and there was great, splashing confusion. And the whales kept up the activity until well after dark. David opened a can of beef stew and ate the whole can—with his shrunken stomach it filled him to bursting—and still the whales tore the bay apart. It was a clear night and half a moon gave light and he watched them, swiveling his head to see one, then another rise and crash back and he realized after a time that he didn't feel alone while they were there. They were more than just something to interest him, they became friends, and when they left, moving and splashing out of the bay in the middle of the night, he watched them with growing sadness.

When he could see them no longer, not even the spouts pluming moisture into the faint moonlight, he raised a hand, standing at the stern holding the boom, and waved with a small motion, a sad little wave and knew, knew then that he could not stay any longer in the bay.

Knew that it was time to go.

He untied the mainsail and pulled it up, then loosened the jib and drew it up as well. Both sails luffed in the night breeze, which was still light and spotty because of the surrounding hills. The anchor had bitten deep as he slept, and he strained on the rope to pull the *Frog* forward and tug the anchor loose. He coiled the rope and chain neatly, as they'd been when he started to anchor, and put them back beneath the captain's bunk. Then he drank some water—the stew had left him thirsty—and went back to the cockpit.

She backed easily in the smooth water, came around and filled quickly. The wind was still out of the north so he ran almost downwind back to the entrance of the bay. It was easy to see the two arms of sand that made the entrance in the moonlight, and he centered between them and almost scooted out of the bay into the open sea.

The swells took the *Frog* immediately. They were larger than when he had come in and had a purpose to them, a rapid movement in spite of their size that almost triggered alarm bells in David's brain. He knew now that swells were telegraph systems, that they came ahead of weather, and that large swells moving this hard and fast probably meant a fair storm.

He thought of turning and going back into the bay to ride it out but decided against it. The storm might be days getting to him, might not come at all, and he didn't have much food and fishing wasn't going that well.

He did not know for certain where he was—except that it was somewhere down along the Baja coast—but he knew that if he didn't sail, didn't move, didn't use the wind and sea he would never get home, and so he hated to just sit.

Once clear of land he brought her around, up into the wind until she was tacking northwest and making a solid six knots. She hit the swells fairly hard, the bow slamming down on every fourth or fifth one, but he held her, heeling well, under full sail for seven hours, until just before dawn, when the storm came.

The storm was different this time.

The swells grew in size at a regular rate, and the wind began to increase but started slowly and worked up at a steady, growing pace.

And David was different now.

He was not panicking, banging around to stow gear below. His mind was steady, his thoughts careful and even.

"We're going to get hit," he said aloud, calmly, talking to the *Frog*. "Let's get ready. . . ."

He let her stop, the sails slapping, went down into the cabin and strung a cord from drawer to drawer to keep them from coming out. Then he lowered the leaves on the table and tied them down, drank some water, tightened the front hatch and went back up.

The wind had increased in strength. He climbed onto the cabin and reefed the main down to half size but left the jib full. Then he went back to the helm, brought her around, and the sails filled and the *Frog* started taking the swells.

There were waves coming now as well, on top of the swells, growing in chop and intensity each moment. The *Frog* was slamming, making noise, but he held her angled up into the wind and took it. Spray came over the bow and covered him, soaking him, but he didn't think he could leave again now and he took it as well—he would not let her do it alone again, not let the sea have her again.

Dawn showed a mean gray sea heading up into leaden gray clouds and a wind that moaned through the stays and rigging. Gusts hit now, like body blows taking her over, but he worked the helm, let her ease up, held her off the wind again and kept the speed between five and six knots, did not run from the storm but into it, used it, rolled with it, absorbed it.

The wind became worse. The waves grew until they were larger than the swells they rode on, towering over him, burying the bow. More than once he was knocked off his feet by a wall of water coming back over the side of the cabin but he never let go of the helm, rose and took it again and again, held her through wave after wave when they rose over him, walls of water, mountains of water moving down on him, down on the *Frog*.

They took it. All that day, slamming, rising, heeling, skidding, slamming down again, up and over and down in the gale—at one point he snarled, growled at the wind and sea—the helm in his gut, his arms aching, his legs on fire; they took it until late day when he sensed a change, felt that the storm was whipped. It had thrown everything it had at them and was now passing.

Inside an hour the wind had lowered from a shriek and the tops of the waves weren't being blown over so hard. In another hour, just before dusk, the main force of the gale was well past them, the waves settling and the wind becoming a good, steady force. He raised the mainsail again to full size and found that she pointed higher yet into the wind, so that he could go a little north of northwest and he was thinking that it felt good to be aimed more for home, was thinking it would be wonderful if he could head straight north and just get home before he ran out of food, however far it was, was thinking of his parents and home and food and the wind and the sea and the storm and how he felt good that he and the *Frog* had taken the storm the way they did to-gether . . .

It was then that he saw the ship—a small, older ship, coming out of the dusk, aiming almost at him but slightly off his bow, running with the wind and sea. Right there. A ship. Right in front of him. She had been running without lights but as soon as the people on deck saw him—there were three of them—they yelled and the lights came on and they started to pass not a hundred yards away, the people waving and yelling and laughing.

For a moment he couldn't say anything. He just didn't think it would happen this way. He didn't know for certain how it would happen, but not this way. Not so sudden. Suddenly he was saved. She was an old, very small coastal freighter but had been fixed up and repainted and she carried an American flag above her bridge.

"Hey," he croaked. They were going to pass him and leave if he didn't wake up. "Hey, hey, hey, hey, *hey*!"

He let go of the helm and waved with both arms, screamed, pointed at them and then at himself and at last they got the message and he heard the engines in the freighter rumble down to a stop west and slightly north of him.

He came about and let the *Frog* sail closer, came up into the wind and stopped about thirty yards away, rising and settling on the waves and swells. He looked up at the people on the rail.

"My name is David Alspeth," he yelled. "I was driven out to sea in a storm. . . ."

"It's him!" one of the young men yelled up at the bridge of the ship. "It's that kid they were searching for up off Ventura." He looked back down at David. "They had your picture in the paper and everything. Man, you are one heck of a distance from where they looked. They finally gave you up for dead, you know that?"

Well, I'm not, David thought. I'm not dead. Not even close. "Where am I?"

The man laughed. "About halfway down the coast of Baja. Maybe two hundred and fifty miles south of San Diego."

Another man came from the bridge, stepping down the ladder, to stand at the rail over the *Frog*. "I am Pierce. Henry Pierce. I am the captain."

David introduced himself—he almost added that he was the captain of the *Frog* but let it be. Captain Pierce was a heavy man, with round shoulders, gray hair, and pleasant eyes. It would sound cocky, smart-mouth to say that he, David, was captain of the *Frog*. But he felt like it.

"You gave everybody a rough time," the captain said. "They had planes and choppers looking for you."

"I was driven way south by the storm," David explained. "Way south . . ."

"Well, you're all right now. We're down here to study whales but we're heading back tomorrow. We'll have you home in three to five days. . . ."

David closed his eyes, sighed, leaned back against the boom with his shoulder. That was it, then. He was done. He was saved. In three to four days he'd be home and there'd be a malt and a hamburger and his mother and father. . . .

"Get your gear," the captain interrupted his dreaming, "anything you want to bring and we'll lower a ladder for you."

David looked up at him. "What about the *Frog*— what about the boat?"

The captain hesitated. "Well . . . we'll have to leave it."

"No." It came out before he could think. Just the word. "No."

The captain of the research vessel shrugged. "We haven't any choice. I haven't got any way to lift it aboard or a place to put it if we did. It's too big."

"No." David shook his head. "We could tow her."

A small smile, a sad smile. "We couldn't pull it more than two or three knots and then it would probably tear the boat apart. Sailboats don't tow at all."

There was a pause; the *Frog* rolled in the swells. The captain stared down at him, the small smile still on his lips. David looked back up at him but wasn't seeing him, wasn't seeing anything; his mind rolled with memories, the shark, the killer whales, the storm, the moon pouring down the sails, the dolphin spinning up into the gold. . . .

All of it in his mind. Then the sentence came. Leave the *Frog*.

Us. We. Leave her to float and die on the ocean. Alone. Leave her to drift and die alone on the ocean.

"No."

"What do you mean, 'no'?" the captain asked.

David shook his head. "I won't leave her. I won't leave the *Frog*."

"But there is no other way. . . ."

"I'll sail her." There, it was out. "I'll sail her home myself. I won't leave her to die . . . to sink. Alone. I'll go back with her."

"You know that it's three hundred and fifty miles back to Ventura? Against prevailing wind and current? You'll have to tack the whole way. It could take two, three weeks. More if you hit bad weather."

David rubbed the wooden boom with one hand. The wood felt warm, smooth, alive. She was alive. The ship had blocked most of the wind but enough flurried around to make the *Frog*'s sails slap a bit and they jerked the boom gently. There was no other way. "I got here with her and I'm going home with her. That's it."

Another long silence while the captain studied him, frowning. A gull which had been following the ship screeched and flew over, banking on a wind eddy.

"I'd do the same," the captain said at last, abruptly, nodding. "By God I'd do the same. Well, is there anything we can do for you, young sailor?"

David thought for a moment. "Two things. First, can you call my parents by radio or something and tell them that I'm all right and that I'll be home . . . well, whenever I get there. Explain everything to them." He gave the captain their phone number.

"Done."

"And the second thing is food and fuel for my stove. I don't have much food left. . . ."

Before he could finish speaking, the other people on the boat, the whale researchers who had been standing silent all this time, started running in different directions and in ten or fifteen minutes had arranged a huge bundle of food and supplies on a blanket which they tied together and lowered to him into the cockpit of the *Frog*. David saw one can peeking through a corner as he put the heavy bundle below in the cabin—the label said it contained a canned chicken. A whole chicken in one can.

"We put in a lot of extra goodies," a girl yelled down, laughing. "Be careful you don't get fat. There's also five gallons of water in a plastic jug."

David thanked them and they talked a little more—the captain told him to stand well off from shore, perhaps a hundred miles, to get good, steady wind—and then it was done. The captain went back up to the bridge, the engines changed their pitch, and the ship slid away into the dusk. As soon as it was clear, the wind hit the *Frog* and David was busy for a few moments trimming the sails and getting her going, and when he turned he could no longer see the ship except for the lights on her radar mast.

He waved once, though he knew they couldn't see it, and returned to work. He would have to get below and put the food away, straighten the cabin up and get everything tight. But the wind was even now, a steady force, and the seas were becoming smaller so the sailing wasn't rough, and the *Frog* hummed to him through the tiller, a song from the water that told him he could stow the food later. Now there was the wind and the sea and the *Frog*.

He had some sailing to do.

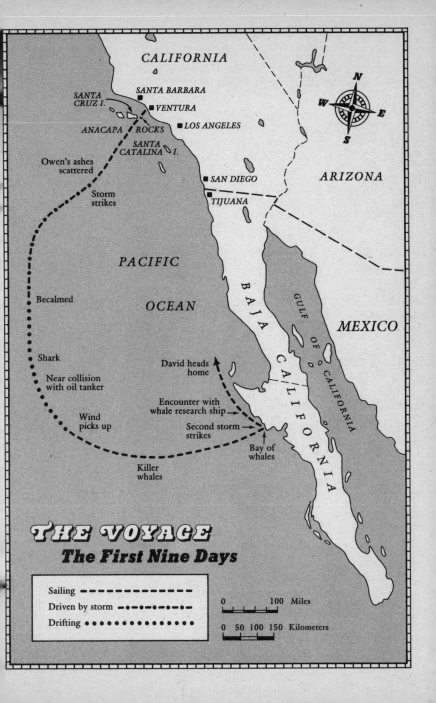